TEACHINGS OF

THE

CHRISTIAN MYSTICS

TEACHINGS

OF THE

CHRISTIAN

MYSTICS

EDITED BY

ANDREW HARVEY

SHAMBHALA

BOSTON & LONDON

1998

Shambhala Publications, Inc.
Horticultural Hall
300 Massachusetts Avenue
Boston, MA 02115
www.shambhala.com

9 8 7 6 5 4 3

Printed in Canada

Book design by Wesley B. Tanner/Passim Editions

♾ This edition is printed on acid-free paper that meets the American
National Standards Institute Z39.48 Standard.

Distributed in the United States by Random House, Inc., and in
Canada by Random House of Canada Ltd

LIBRARY OF CONGRESS CATALOGING-IN PUBLICATIONS DATA

Teachings of the Christian mystics/edited by Andrew Harvey.
        p.   cm.
    ISBN 1-57062-343-0 (pbk.)
    1. Mysticism.   I. Harvey, Andrew, 1952–
BV5082.2.T43 1998
248.2'2—dc21
                                            97-22297
                                            CIP

FOR CAROLINE BOUTERAON
WITH ALL MY LOVE
& GRATITUDE

Jesus said, "Whoever drinks from
my mouth will become like me;
I myself shall become that person,
and the hidden things will be
revealed to him."

Logion 108
Gospel of Thomas

Contents

———

ACKNOWLEDGMENTS

—

To my husband, Eryk, for the example of his devotion to the Virgin, and his love.

To Maria Todisco, whose tireless help, encouragement, and profound spiritual intelligence helped birth this work.

To my dear friend and true Christian, Mollie Corcoran.

To Leila and Henry Luce, for their warmth and kindness.

To Anne Pennington, who prayed and believed.

To Peter Levi, who inspired.

To Mary Ford-Grabowski, for the truth of her heart.

To my beloved friend-in-God, Bede Griffiths, who showed me the way home.

INTRODUCTION

There is nothing more important, I believe, for the future of the mystical renaissance that is struggling to be born everywhere in the West — and thus for the future of the planet — than an authentic and unsparing recovery of the full range, power, and glory of the Christian mystical tradition. Without such a recovery, the spiritual life of the West will continue to be a superficial, narcissistic, and sometimes lethal mixture of a watered-down or fanatical pseudo-Christianity, hardly understood "eastern" metaphysics, and regressive occultism — and the great radical potential of such a renaissance will go unlived and unenacted, with disastrous consequences for every human being and for all of nature.

What is needed is the flaming-out, on a global scale, of an unstoppable force of Divine-human love wise enough to stay in permanent humble contact with the Divine and brave enough to call for, risk, and implement change at every level and in every arena before time runs out and we destroy ourselves. Such a love has to spring from an awakened mystical consciousness, and must be rooted in habits of fervent meditation, adoration of the Divine, and prayer; for only then will it be illuminated enough to act at all times with healing courage, and strong enough to withstand the ordeals and torments that are inevitable. Teilhard de Chardin wrote, "Some day, after we have mastered the winds, the waves, the tides and gravity, . . . we shall harness the energies of love. Then, for the second time in the history of the world, man will have discovered fire." Unless humankind discovers this fire, and uses it to burn away everything that blocks the changes that must come in order to transform the planet into the mirror of divine beauty in is meant to be, it will die out and take most of nature with it.

At the core of Christ's enterprise is an experience of this fire and the revolutionary passion of charity that blazes from it. This passion, as Christ knew and lived it, cannot rest until it has burnt down all the divisions that separate one human heart from another and so from reality. No authority except that of the Divine, is sacred to it; no dogma, however hallowed, that keeps oppression of any kind alive can withstand the onslaught of its flame. All of human experience, personal and political, is arraigned and exposed by it. It demands of everyone who approaches it a loving and humble submission to its fierce, mind and heart shattering power and a commitment to enact its laws of radical compassion and hunger for justice in every arena. Its aim is the irradiation of all of life with holy and vibrant energy and truth, so that as many beings as possible can live, here on earth and in the body, in a direct relationship with God, each other, and nature, in what Saint Paul unforgettably calls "the glorious liberty of the Children of God."

Many forces, even within the "Christian" world, block the unleashing of this "glorious liberty." Anyone who comes to feel even a small spark of the heat of this fire may look in vain to find any of its truth in the churches that claim to keep it alive. Fundamentalism of any kind is alien to its adoration of freedom and its all-embracing love of all beings and all creation; the narrow judgmental ethics that disfigure all denominations of Christianity represent precisely that separation that Christ himself wanted to end forever. Most Western seekers are refugees from hypocritical, patriarchal, misogynistic, and homophobic versions of Christ's message that are tantamount to perverse, even demonic, betrayals of it. The great mystical treasures of all the Christian traditions have been largely ignored for centuries, even in the monastic institutions that might have kept them alive. With such a grim prospect, it is hardly surprising that many seekers continue to project onto Christ and his teachings only what they learned from suffering the mutilation of both by the churches. The majority of Westerners interested in spiritual transformation and aware of its necessity know very little about the Christian mystics; they know more about the Hindu or Sufi or Buddhist mystical traditions than about the one that is the hidden and glorious secret of their own civilization. Many more have read the *Bhagavad Gita* or Rumi than have read Ruusbroec or Jacopone da Todi or Saint John of the Cross; many more have practiced *vipassana* or *bhakti* yoga than have attempted the spiritual exercises of Ignatius of Loyola or than have prayed the Jesus Prayer with Symeon the New Theologian and Nicephorus the Solitary. The result is that the explosive force of Christ's subversion of all forms of authority and all forms of worldly power goes largely unnoticed, and a vast power for fundamental change on every level goes unused.

This is a tragedy because, of all the mystic pioneers of humanity, Christ is in almost every way the most daring and demanding and the most concerned with the brutal facts of this world. His living out of his enlightenment and his realization of his fundamental unity with God has an unique urgency, a poignantly wild passion, and a hunger for justice that make him the hero of love in the human race. Christ came not to found a new religion or to inaugurate a new set of dogmas but to open up a fierce and shattering new path of love-in-action, a path that seems now, with the hindsight of history, the one that could have saved — and still could save — humanity from its course of suicidal self-destruction.

At the moment when the patriarchy was beginning its long, dark triumph in the form of the Roman Empire, Christ revealed and enacted a way of being completely subversive to all of its beliefs and "truths." To a world obsessed by power, he offered a vision of the radiance of powerlessness and the powerful vulnerability of love; to a culture riddled with authoritarianism, false pomp, and greed he gave a vision of the holiness of inner and outer poverty and a critique of the vanity and horror of all forms of worldly achievement so scalding that most of his own followers have contrived every means imaginable to ignore it. To a society arranged at every level into oppressive hierarchies — sexual, religious, racial, and political — he presented in his own life, a vision of a radical and all-embracing egalitarianism designed to end forever those dogmas and institutions that keep women enslaved, the poor starving, and the rich rotting in a prison of selfish luxury. In his own life, he showed what the new life this path would open up to everyone who risked its rigors would be like — how free and tender and brave and charged with healing ecstatic power. Faithful always to the humble egalitarianism of his understanding of divine love, he refused all the glamour of sagedom, constantly undermining all of the fantasies that others tried to project onto him, and he finally embraced horrible and humiliating suffering on the Cross to break through into that dimension of Resurrection and cosmic life from which he continues to guide, enflame, and inspire all who turn to him.

So demanding and illusionless a path remains a perpetual challenge to anyone who dares to see its truth. This truth in its fullness was almost immediately betrayed by the historical development of Christianity. An egalitarian path that welcomed and celebrated women was turned into a hierarchical and misogynistic Church; a vision that criticized all power was conscripted to sustain first imperial and then papal ambitions; a force of love that wanted to end all division and separation became a force of fanaticism and fundamentalism that derided other religions and created one more prison of exclusion. A force of Wholeness — Christ was never an ascetic and never denigrated the body or sexuality — became a force of alienation, separating body from soul, man from woman, humanity from nature, and privileging renunciation and celibacy as the surest way to God.

As an integral part of this betrayal, Christ himself was

dogmatically separated from the human race he wanted to liberate. He was declared the Son of God, a perfect being whose divinity set him apart from everyone. Christ himself never claimed to be Son of God; his only claim, significantly, was to be "Son of Man." It is clear that Christ did not wish to be worshipped as a God; he wanted, in fact, to do something far more necessary and far more subversive — to reveal, by living it, the divine truth of every human identity and so instruct and empower the Christ within each of us and bring each of us into the atmosphere and splendor of the Kingdom of God that is our natural and rightful inheritance. Declaring Christ unique and divine muted the outrageousness of Christ's real adventure and created a subtle chasm between humanity and him that prevented the full liberating power of his radical discovery of the divine power and truth latent in everyone from reaching and transforming the world. As Jung wrote,

> The demand made by the *Imitatio Christi*, that we should follow this ideal and seek to become like it, ought logically to have the result of developing and exalting the inner man. In actual fact, however, the ideal has been turned by superficial and formalistically minded believers into an external object of worship, and it is precisely this veneration of the object that pre-

vents it from reaching down into the depths of the soul and transforming it into a wholeness in keeping with the ideal. Accordingly, the divine mediator stands outside as an image, while man remains fragmentary and untouched in the deepest part of him.

In the great Christian mystics, however, we can read the words of those who, whatever they may have believed about Christ's unique divinity, did not remain "fragmentary and untouched" in the deepest part of themselves, but staked their lives not merely on following some version of Christ's teaching but on submitting themselves to the same almost intolerable pressures, vicissitudes, and passions as he had so as to be "Christed" with him. For them, Christ was more than a teacher or sage or even Divine image; he was the pioneer of a wholly new kind of human being, one who wanted to become one with the fire of love and to be its selfless revolutionary in the dark night of human history. Brave and loving enough — and constantly inspired by divine Grace — these heroic men and women took up Christ's challenge — the challenge, above all, of the Cross — and allowed themselves, like him, to be crucified unto Resurrection, killed unto an eternal life dedicated utterly to love and the service of others. Despite often terrible opposition from the Church of their day — and all forms of scandal and humiliation — they did not dishonor their great brother, and kept the flame of his spiritual truth and of the new being it births alive.

When the Christian mystical tradition is seen in its entirety — and I hope this anthology will do something to enable this — what will, I believe, become most clear is the radically subversive and sobering nature of its humility — a humility that springs directly from the explosive and deranging example of Christ himself. Christ's enlightenment has nothing safe or omnipotent about it; its symbol is not a triumph of effortlessness but one of utter and devastating self-gift: the Cross. Again and again, Christ, in his teachings and by his example, made it clear that the only authentic sign of spiritual wisdom is a progress in the kind of ego-annihilating humility that longs to express itself in the ever-greater and richer service of all beings. There is nothing to comfort the ordinary or subtle spiritual ego in this stark vision, no place for any kind of pride or grandiosity to hide; Christ made this eternally clear when he himself, as one of his final acts among them before his Passion, washed the feet of his disciples. In the Christ-path, the richest are those who give the most; the highest are those who lovingly take the lowest place; those who really love God prove it in unstinting service to human beings and the creation, and willingly embrace whatever suffering standing for justice and mercy in a vicious world must bring and whatever ordeal is necessary for their inner purification. Christ himself gave, humbly, everything; those who approach the fire of his love slowly learn the force and demand of his terrible humility.

I believe that seekers of every kind have four essential, exacting, and sobering lessons to learn from the terrible humility of the tradition of Christ, lessons that echo again and again through the pages of this book. The first is that even in the highest and final stages of mystical illumination — even in the "spiritual marriage" of Teresa of Ávila or Johannes Ruusbroec — a crucial gap still remains between Creator and creature that necessitates a continuing practice of prayer, contemplation, and service; oneness with God in love is possible, but not in nature and being. Even in the inner lives of the greatest saints and mystics, there is always still work to be done, for the demand and power of divine love are infinite and endless. Christ himself, though one with God in love, never stopped growing to incarnate more and more of that love. All those who love and follow him submit to the same ruthless laws of continual transformation.

Such a vision permanently humbles all spiritual pride and leads to the second great radical insight of the Christian mystical tradition — that enshrined in Gregory of Nyssa's vision of the doctrine of infinite growth ("*epecta-*

sis"). In this vision, entering the force-field of the Christ consciousness opens up the possibility of infinite expansion and change. Consequently, for the Christian mystic, enlightenment is not in any sense a static state of omniscience or oneness with being as the eastern religions have tended to represent it — but a continual opening up to and evolution in love. No being, even in the highest angelic hierarchies, can claim to be *wholly* wise or *wholly* transformed; there are always new mountains of gnosis and adoration to climb. Such a vision simultaneously exalts and humbles — exalts because it reveals the law of an evolution without end in every arena and dimension of the universe, humbles because it shows clearly that the prerequisite for such growth is a continual self-donation to an always-higher and always-transcendent power.

Christ and those who followed (and follow) him also teach us a third humbling lesson: that the price for such infinite growth and expansion in love is, as Christ's own terrifying life makes clear, a heroic embrace of the laws of suffering and ordeal. To accept the demands of love is to accept the Cross and the extreme suffering that comes with it. Authentic divine love, Saint Francis said, "suffers as a bird sings": there is no way out of such suffering and it is the peculiar noble greatness of Christ and his lovers that they never wanted a way out. There are no greater teachers of the purpose and alchemical power of suffering in any other mystical literature, because no other group of mystics have faced the necessity of ordeal with such unshrinking precision and so learned how to transmute agony into thanksgiving; or even, in the highest and rarest cases, like Christ himself, fuse them in one continual out-pouring of love. The insights of such alchemists of horror are priceless, I believe, at a time when all seekers are called on to transform themselves extremely fast to be of use in a devastated world. To work for a new humanity in a world as violent and corrupt as ours must involve great pain and frightening vulnerability to derision, even perse-cution, and the temptation to despair: the Christian tradi-tion explores the healing paradoxes of ordeal in a way that can embolden and instruct everyone.

The fourth humbling lesson that Christ and his mysti-cal brothers and sisters teach us is that no mystical train-ing is authentic unless it results in a total commitment to other beings and to the service of justice and compassion in all forms in the creation. There is nothing world-aban-doning about greatest of the Christian mystics; they strive to incarnate that electric balance between contemplation of God and action in reality that characterized Christ him-self. The tremendous danger that the world is in demands all of us that we learn to fuse at every level the deepest possible contemplative connection to the Divine with the most precise and responsible possible action in reality so the world can be constantly infused with the creativity and justice of God. We have everything to learn from Christ and the Christian mystics on how most effectively and humbly to do this.

What I hope this anthology will also make clear is that the conventional picture of Christianity as essentially a patriarchal, life-denying, world-despising religion is a travesty — one for which, of course, the churches are largely responsible. The truth is that the authentic Christian tradition, and Christ's teaching itself, is everywhere saturated with the healing and life-affirming truths of the sacred feminine, and with its wisdom of sensitivity, tenderness, and honoring of all life, and its respect for the necessity of suffering and vulnerability. Inept translation and patriarchal distortion of what Christ said and did have obscured this truth — and with it a great deal of the transforming and radical power of Christ-consciousness.

The clue to its full recovery, I believe, as I have written in my book *Return of the Mother*, is the full recovery of the mystical role in the birth of Christ-consciousness of Mary the Mother. Until Mary is seen in her full glory, as the incarnation of the Divine Motherhood of God, Christ cannot be seen in his, because he is as much the son of the

Mother, the apostle of the transforming powers and life-rich truths of the sacred feminine, as he is the Son of the Father. Christ's experience of the Divine was a complete experience of the Mother aspect of God as well as that of God-the-Father. It is this completeness that gives his life and teaching such all-embracing authority and such a miraculous fusion of transcendent adoration and immanent concern, of the fiercest clarity and intellectual power with the most acute tenderness for all life.

One of the greatest mysteries of the Christian mystical tradition is how the awareness of Mary's essential role in the transformation of love that Christ came to effect has expanded astonishingly over the centuries. This anthology celebrates this discovery of the power of Divine Motherhood in Mary in all of its crucial stages — from the explosion of interest in and adoration of her in the fourth and fifth centuries (represented here in two excerpts from the Akathist Hymn of Romanos the Melodist), through the great upsurge of devotion to her in the Middle Ages (whose pioneer and architect was Bernard of Clairvaux) to the prophetic work in the early eighteenth century of Louis Marie Grignion de Montfort, whom I consider to be the greatest of all Marian mystics and the one who gives us all the deepest and greatest clues as to the authentic meaning of the second coming when he writes:

It is through the very Holy Virgin that Jesus Christ came into the world to begin with, and it is also through her that he will reign in the world. . . . until now, the divine Mary has been unknown, and this is one of the reasons why Jesus Christ is hardly known as he should be. If then — as is certain — the knowledge and reign of Jesus Christ arrive in the world it will be a necessary consequence of the knowledge and reign of the very Holy Virgin, who birthed him into this world the first time and will make him burst out everywhere the second.

De Montfort is announcing a great mystical truth; that the Christ consciousness, in all its tenderness and radical passion, is born from as complete as possible an adoration of the sacred feminine. In the last hundred and fifty years, the Virgin has been appearing all over the world, warning humanity of the danger of living without God and without love and trying to open all beings to the truths of the Heart. She has been, as the mystical Mother of all new beings, preparing the ground for the birth of the Christ in all of us, through wonder, prayer, unconditional love, and unstinting service. At the potential end of history Mother and Son then, are returning in a new and revolutionary dance of love and wisdom whose consequences could be — if we allow them to — completely transforming.

The Second Coming will not, I believe, be the return of Christ as a figure: that version perpetuates the old deification of Christ that has kept his force inert in history. The *real* Second Coming will be the birthing of Christ-consciousness in millions of beings who turn, in the Father-Mother, towards the fire of love and take the supreme risk of incarnating divine love-in-action on Earth. This Second Coming could potentially alter the level of consciousness of the whole of humanity and initiate it into that mystical wisdom that it desperately needs if its problems are going to be solved.

May all those who come to this book be inspired to allow themselves to be "birthed" into love and so serve humbly and with undauntable love the future of humankind.

TEACHINGS OF
THE
CHRISTIAN MYSTICS

THE KINGDOM OF HEAVEN

The kingdom of heaven is like to a grain of mustard seed, which a man took, and sowed in his field:

Which indeed is the least of all seeds: but when it is grown, it is the greatest among herbs, and becometh a tree, so that the birds of the air come and lodge in the branches thereof.

The kingdom of heaven is like unto leaven, which a woman took, and hid in three measures of meal, till the whole was leavened.

Again, the kingdom of heaven is like unto treasure hid in a field; the which when a man hath found, he hideth, and for joy thereof goeth and selleth all that he hath, and buyeth that field.

Again, the kingdom of heaven is like unto a merchant man, seeking goodly pearls:

Who, when he had found one pearl of great price, went and sold all that he had, and bought it.

Matthew 13:31–33, 44–46 (AV)

The Sermon on the Mount

And seeing the multitudes, he went up into a mountain: and when he was set, his disciples came unto him:
And he opened his mouth, and taught them, saying,
"Blessed are the poor in spirit: for theirs is the kingdom of heaven.

"Blessed are they that mourn: for they shall be comforted.

"Blessed are the meek: for they shall inherit the earth.

"Blessed are they which do hunger and thirst after righteousness: for they shall be filled.

"Blessed are the merciful: for they shall obtain mercy.

"Blessed are the pure in heart: for they shall see God.

"Blessed are the peacemakers: for they shall be called the children of God.

"Blessed are they which are persecuted for righteousness' sake: for theirs is the kingdom of heaven.

"Blessed are ye, when men shall revile you, and persecute you, and shall say all manner of evil against you falsely, for my sake.

"Rejoice, and be exceedingly glad: for great is your

reward in heaven: for so persecuted they the prophets which were before you.

"Ye are the salt of the earth: but if the salt have lost his savour, wherewith shall it be salted? It is thenceforth good for nothing, but to be cast out, and to be trodden under foot of men.

"Ye are the light of the world. A city that is set on an hill cannot be hid.

"Neither do men light a candle, and put it under a bushel, but on a candlestick; and it giveth light unto all that are in the house.

"Let your light so shine before men, that they may see your good works, and glorify your Father which is in heaven."

Matthew 5:1–16 (AV)

Be Ye Therefore Perfect

Ye have heard that it hath been said, An eye for an eye, and a tooth for a tooth:

But I say unto you, That ye resist not evil: but whosoever shall smite thee on thy right cheek, turn to him the other also.

And if any man will sue thee at the law, and take away thy coat, let him have thy cloak also.

And whosoever shall compel thee to go a mile, go with him twain.

Give to him that asketh thee, and from him that would borrow of thee turn not thou away.

Ye have heard that it hath been said, Thou shalt love thy neighbor, and hate thine enemy.

But I say unto you, Love your enemies, bless them that curse you, do good to them that hate you, and pray for them which despitefully use you, and persecute you;

That ye may be the children of your Father which is in heaven; for he maketh his sun to rise on the evil and on the good, and sendeth rain on the just and on the unjust.

For if ye love them which love you, what reward have ye? do not even the publicans the same?

And if ye salute your brethren only, what do ye more than others? do not even the publicans so?

Be ye therefore perfect, even as your Father which is in heaven is perfect.

Matthew 5:38–48 (AV)

Seek Ye First the Kingdom of God

Lay not up for yourselves treasures upon earth, where moth and rust doth corrupt, and where thieves break through and steal:

But lay up for yourselves treasures in heaven, where neither moth nor rust doth corrupt, and where thieves do not break through nor steal:

For where your treasure is, there will your heart be also.

The light of the body is the eye: if therefore thine eye be single, thy whole body shall be full of light. . . .

No man can serve two masters: for either he will hate the one, and love the other; or else he will hold to the one, and despise the other. Ye cannot serve God and mammon.

Therefore I say unto you, Take no thought for your life, what ye shall eat, or what ye shall drink; not yet for your body, what ye shall put on. Is not the life more than meat, and the body than raiment?

Behold the fowls of the air: for they sow not, neither do they reap, nor gather into barns; yet your heavenly Father feedeth them. Are ye not much better than they?

Which of you by taking thought can add one cubit unto his stature?

And why take ye thought for raiment? Consider the lilies of the field, how they grow; they toil not, neither do they spin:

And yet I say unto you, That even Solomon in all his glory was not arrayed like one of these.

Wherefore, if God so clothe the grass of the field, which today is, and tomorrow is cast into the oven, shall he not much more clothe you, O ye of little faith?

Therefore take no thought, saying, What shall we eat? or, What shall we drink? or, Wherewithal shall we be clothed?

(For after all these things do the Gentiles seek:) for your heavenly Father knoweth that ye have need of all these things.

But seek ye first the kingdom of God, and his right-eousness; and all these things shall be added unto you.

Matthew 6:19–22, 24–33 (AV)

Ask and It Shall Be Given

Ask, and it shall be given you; seek, and ye shall find; knock, and it shall be opened unto you:

For every one that asketh receiveth; and he that seeketh findeth; and to him that knocketh it shall be opened.

Or what man is there of you, whom if his son ask bread, will he give him a stone?

Or if he ask a fish, will he give him a serpent?

If ye then, being evil, know how to give good gifts unto your children, how much more shall your Father which is in heaven give good things to them that ask him?

Therefore all things whatsoever ye would that men should do to you, do ye even so to them: for this is the law and the prophets.

Matthew 7:7–12 (AV)

I Was Thirsty
and You Gave Me Drink

When the Son of man shall come in his glory, and all the holy angels with him, then shall he sit upon the throne of his glory:

And before him shall be gathered all nations: and he shall separate them one from another, as a shepherd divideth his sheep from the goats:

And he shall set the sheep on his right hand, but the goats on the left.

Then shall the King say unto them on his right hand, "Come, ye blessed of my Father, inherit the kingdom prepared for you from the foundation of the world:

"For I was an hungered, and ye gave me meat: I was thirsty, and ye gave me drink: I was a stranger, and ye took me in:

"Naked, and ye clothed me: I was sick, and ye visited me: I was in prison, and ye came unto me."

Then shall the righteous answer him, saying, "Lord, when saw we thee an hungered, and fed thee? or thirsty, and gave thee drink?

"When saw we thee a stranger, and took thee in? or naked, and clothed thee?

"Or when saw we thee sick, or in prison, and came unto thee?"

And the King shall answer and say unto them, "Verily I say unto you, Inasmuch as ye have done it unto one of the least of these my brethren, ye have done it unto me."

Then shall he say also unto them on the left hand, "Depart from me, ye cursed, into everlasting fire, prepared for the devil and his angels:

"For I was an hungered, and ye gave me no meat: I was thirsty, and ye gave me no drink:

"I was a stranger, and ye took me not in: naked, and ye clothed me not: sick, and in prison, and ye visited me not."

Then shall they also answer him, saying, "Lord, when saw we thee an hungered, or athirst, or a stranger, or naked, or sick, or in prison, and did not minister unto thee?"

Then shall he answer them, saying, "Verily I say unto you, Inasmuch as ye did it not to one of the least of these, ye did it not to me."

Matthew 25:31–45 (AV)

TAKE UP YOUR CROSS

And when he had called the people unto him with his disciples also, he said unto them, "Whosoever will come after me, let him deny himself, and take up his cross, and follow me.

"For whosoever will save his life shall lose it; but whosoever shall lose his life for my sake and the gospel's, the same shall save it.

"For what shall it profit a man, if he shall gain the whole world, and lose his own soul?"

Mark 8:34–36 (AV)

BE AS A LITTLE CHILD

And they brought young children to him, that he should touch them: and his disciples rebuked those that brought them.

But when Jesus saw it, he was much displeased, and said unto them, "Suffer the little children to come unto me, and forbid them not: for of such is the kingdom of God.

"Verily I say unto you, Whosoever shall not receive the kingdom of God as a little child, he shall not enter therein."

Mark 10:13–15 (AV)

More Than All Burnt Offerings
and Sacrifices

And one of the scribes came, . . . and . . . asked him, "Which is the first commandment of all?"

And Jesus answered him, "The first of all the commandments is, Hear, O Israel; The Lord our God is one Lord:

And thou shalt love the Lord thy God with all thy heart, and with all thy soul, and with all thy mind, and with all thy strength: this is the first commandment.

"And the second is like, namely this, Thou shalt love thy neighbour as thyself. There is none other commandment greater than these."

And the scribe said unto him, "Well, Master, thou hast said the truth: for there is one God; and there is none other but he:

"And to love him with all the heart and with all the understanding, and with all the soul, and with all the strength, and to love his neighbour as himself, is more than all whole burnt offerings and sacrifices."

And when Jesus saw that he answered discreetly, he said unto him, "Thou art not far from the kingdom of God."

Mark 12:28–34 (AV)

YE MUST BE BORN AGAIN

Except a man be born of water and of the Spirit, he cannot enter into the kingdom of God.

That which is born of the flesh is flesh; and that which is born of the Spirit is spirit.

Marvel not that I said unto thee, Ye must be born again.

The wind bloweth where it listeth, and thou hearest the sound thereof, but canst not tell whence it cometh, and whither it goeth: so is every one that is born of the Spirit.

John 3:5–8 (AV)

The Coming of the Holy Spirit, the Comforter

If ye love me, keep my commandments.

And I will pray the Father, and he shall give you another Comforter, that he may abide with you for ever;

Even the Spirit of truth; whom the world cannot receive, because it seeth him not, neither knoweth him: but ye know him; for he dwelleth with you, and shall be in you.

I will not leave you comfortless: I will come to you.

Yet a little while, and the world seeth me no more; but ye see me: because I live, ye shall live also.

At that day ye shall know that I am in my Father, and ye in me, and I in you.

He that hath my commandments, and keepeth them, he it is that loveth me: and he that loveth me shall be loved of my Father, and I will love him, and will manifest myself to him. . . .

These things I have spoken unto you, being yet present with you.

But the Comforter, which is the Holy Ghost, whom the

Father will send in my name, he shall teach you all things, and bring all things to your remembrance, whatsoever I have said unto you.

Peace I leave with you, my peace I give unto you: not as the world giveth, give I unto you. Let not your heart be troubled, neither let it be afraid.

John 14:15–21, 25–27 (AV)

The Vine

I am the true vine, and my Father is the husbandman.

Every branch in me that beareth not fruit he taketh away: and every branch that beareth fruit, he purgeth it, that it may bring forth more fruit.

Now ye are clean through the word which I have spoken unto you.

Abide in me, and I in you. As the branch cannot bear fruit of itself, except it abide in the vine; no more can ye, except ye abide in me.

I am the vine, ye are the branches: He that abideth in me, and I in him, the same bringeth forth much fruit: for without me ye can do nothing.

If a man abide not in me, he is cast forth as a branch, and is withered; and men gather them, and cast them into the fire, and they are burned.

If ye abide in me, and my words abide in you, ye shall ask what ye will, and it shall be done unto you.

Herein is my Father glorified, that ye bear much fruit; so shall ye be my disciples.

As the Father hath loved me, so have I loved you: continue ye in my love.

If ye keep my commandments, ye shall abide in my love; even as I have kept my Father's commandments, and abide in his love.

These things have I spoken unto you, that my joy might remain in you, and that your joy might be full.

John 15:1–11 (AV)

I in Them and Thou in Me

Jesus . . . lifted up his eyes to heaven, and said, "Father, the hour is come; glorify thy Son, that thy Son also may glorify thee:

"As thou hast given him power over all flesh, that he should give eternal life to as many as thou hast given him.

"And this is life eternal, that they might know thee the only true God, and Jesus Christ, whom thou has sent.

"I have glorified thee on the earth: I have finished the work which thou gavest me to do.

"And now, O Father, glorify thou me with thine own self with the glory which I had with thee before the world was.

"I have manifested thy name unto the men which thou gavest me out of the world: thine they were, and thou gavest them me; and they have kept thy word. . . .

"Neither pray I for these alone, but for them also which shall believe on me through their word;

"That they all may be one; as thou, Father, art in me, and I in thee, that they also may be one in us: that the world may believe that thou hast sent me.

"And the glory which thou gavest me I have given them; that they may be one, even as we are one:

"I in them, and thou in me, that they may be made perfect in one; and that the world may know that thou hast sent me, and hast loved them, as thou hast loved me.

"Father, I will that they also, whom thou hast given me, be with me where I am; that they may behold my glory, which thou hast given me: for thou lovedst me before the foundation of the world.

"O righteous Father, the world hath not known thee: but I have known thee, and these have known that thou hast sent me.

"And I have declared unto them thy name, and will declare it: that the love wherewith thou hast loved me may be in them, and I in them."

John 17:1–6, 20–26 (AV)

IF YOU WILL NOT KNOW YOURSELVES

If your leaders say to you,
"Look, the kingdom is in the sky,"
then the birds of the sky will precede you.
If they say to you,
"it is in the sea,"
then the fish will precede you.

Rather,
the kingdom is inside of you,
and it is outside of you.

When you come to know yourselves,
then you will become known,
and you will realize that it is you
who are the sons of the living Father.

But if you will not know yourselves,
you dwell in poverty,
and it is you who are that poverty.

Logion 3, Gospel of Thomas

The Sign of the Father

If they say to you,
"Where did you come from?"
Say to them,
"We came from the light,
"The place where light came into being
"Of its own accord
"And established itself
"And became manifested through their image."

If they say to you,
"Is it you?"
Say,
"We are its children,
"And we are the elect of the Living Father."

If they ask you,
"What is the sign of your Father in you?"
Say to them,
"It is movement and repose."

Logion 50, Gospel of Thomas

Into a Single One

Jesus saw some babies nursing.
He said to his disciples:
"These babies nursing are like those
Who enter the kingdom."
His disciples said to him:
"Shall we then enter the kingdom as babies?"
Jesus answered them and said:
"When you make the two into one,
"And when you make the inner like the outer,
"And the outer like the inner,
"And the upper like the lower,
"And when you make male and female
"Into a single one,
"So that the male will not be male
"And the female not be female . . .
"Then you shall enter the kingdom."

Logion 22, Gospel of Thomas

We Are the Children of God

The Spirit itself beareth witness with our spirit, that we are the children of God:

And if children, then heirs; heirs of God, and joint-heirs with Christ; if so be that we suffer with him, that we may also be glorified together.

For I reckon that the sufferings of this present time are not worthy to be compared with the glory which shall be revealed in us.

For the earnest expectation of the creature waiteth for the manifestation of the sons of God.

For the creature was made subject to vanity, not willingly, but by reason of him who hath subjected the same in hope,

Because the creature itself also shall be delivered from the bondage of corruption into the glorious liberty of the children of God.

For we know that the whole creation groaneth and travaileth in pain together until now.

And not only they, but ourselves also, which have the

first fruits of the Spirit, even we ourselves groan within ourselves, waiting for the adoption, to wit, the redemption of our body.

St. Paul, Romans 8:16–23 (AV)

BE YE TRANSFORMED

I beseech you therefore, brethren, by the mercies of God, that ye present your bodies a living sacrifice, holy, acceptable unto God, which is your reasonable service.

And be not conformed to this world: but be ye transformed by the renewing of your mind, that ye may prove what is that good, and acceptable, and perfect, will of God.

For I say, through the grace given unto me, to every man that is among you, not to think of himself more highly than he ought to think; but to think soberly, according as God hath dealt to every man the measure of faith.

For as we have many members in one body, and all members have not the same office:

So we, being many, are one body in Christ, and every one members one of another.

Having then gifts differing according to the grace that is given to us, whether prophecy, let us prophesy according to the proportion of faith;

Or ministry, let us wait on our ministering: or he that teacheth, on teaching;

Or he that exhorteth, on exhortation: he that giveth, let

him do it with simplicity; he that ruleth, with diligence; he that sheweth mercy, with cheerfulness.

Let love be without dissimulation. Abhor that which is evil; cleave to that which is good.

St. Paul, Romans 12:1–9 (AV)

When I Am Weak,
Then I Am Strong

I knew a man in Christ above fourteen years ago, (whether in the body, I cannot tell; or whether out of the body, I cannot tell: God knoweth;) such an one caught up to the third heaven.

And I knew such a man, (whether in the body, or out of the body, I cannot tell: God knoweth;)

How that he was caught up into paradise, and heard unspeakable words, which it is not lawful for a man to utter.

Of such an one will I glory: yet of myself I will not glory, but in mine infirmities.

For though I would desire to glory, I shall not be a fool; for I will say the truth: but now I forbear, lest any man should think of me above that which he seeth me to be, or that he heareth of me.

And lest I should be exalted above measure through the abundance of the revelations, there was given to me a thorn in the flesh, the messenger of Satan to buffet me, lest I should be exalted above measure.

For this thing I besought the Lord thrice, that it might depart from me.

And he said unto me, My grace is sufficient for thee: for my strength is made perfect in weakness. Most gladly therefore will I rather glory in my infirmities, that the power of Christ may rest upon me.

Therefore I take pleasure in infirmities, in reproaches, in necessities, in persecutions, in distresses for Christ's sake: for when I am weak, then am I strong.

II Corinthians 12:2–10

The Foolishness of God
Is Wiser Than Men

For the preaching of the cross is to them that perish foolishness; but unto us which are saved it is the power of God.

For it is written, I will destroy the wisdom of the wise, and will bring to nothing the understanding of the prudent.

Where is the wise? where is the scribe? where is the disputer of this world? hath not God made foolish the wisdom of this world?

For after that in the wisdom of God the world by wisdom knew not God, it pleased God by the foolishness of preaching to save them that believe.

For the Jews require a sign, and the Greeks seek after wisdom:

But we preach Christ crucified, unto the Jews a stumbling block, and unto the Greeks foolishness;

But unto them which are called, both Jews and Greeks, Christ the power of God, and the wisdom of God.

Because the foolishness of God is wiser than men; and the weakness of God is stronger than men.

For ye see your calling, brethren, how that not many wise men after the flesh, not many mighty, not many noble are called:

But God hath chosen the foolish things of the world to confound the wise; and God hath chosen the weak things of the world to confound the things which are mighty;

And base things of the world, and things which are despised, hath God chosen, yea, and things which are not, to bring to nought things that are:

That no flesh should glory in his presence. . . .

Let no man deceive himself. If any man among you seemeth to be wise in this world, let him become a fool, that he may be wise.

For the wisdom of this world is foolishness with God. For it is written, He taketh the wise in their own craftiness.

And again, The Lord knoweth the thoughts of the wise, that they are vain.

Therefore let no man glory in men. For all things are yours;

Whether Paul, or Apollos, or Cephas, or the world, or life, or death, or things present, or things to come; all are yours;

And ye are Christ's; and Christ is God's.

St. Paul; I Corinthians 1:18–29, 3:18–23 (AV)

I Count Not Myself
to Have Apprehended

But what things were gain to me, those I counted loss for Christ.

Yea doubtless, and I count all things but loss for the excellency of the knowledge of Christ Jesus my Lord: for whom I have suffered the loss of all things, and do count them but dung, that I may win Christ,

And be found in him, not having mine own righteousness, which is of the law, but that which is through the faith of Christ, the righteousness which is of God by faith:

That I may know him, and the power of his resurrection, and the fellowship of his sufferings, being made comformable unto his death;

If by any means I might attain unto the resurrection of the dead.

Not as though I had already attained, either were already perfect: but I follow after, if that I may apprehend that for which also I am apprehended of Christ Jesus.

Brethren, I count not myself to have apprehended: but this one thing I do, forgetting those things which are behind, and reaching forth unto those things which are before,

I press toward the mark for the prize of the high calling of God in Christ Jesus.

Let us therefore, as many as be perfect, be thus minded: and if in any thing ye be otherwise minded, God shall reveal even this unto you.

St. Paul, Philippians 3:7–15 (AV)

The Glory of Charity

Though I speak with the tongues of men and of angels, and have not charity, I am become as sounding brass, or a tinkling cymbal.

And though I have the gift of prophecy, and understand all mysteries, and all knowledge; and though I have all faith, so that I could remove mountains, and have not charity, I am nothing.

And though I bestow all my goods to feed the poor, and though I give my body to be burned, and have not charity, it profiteth me nothing.

Charity suffereth long, and is kind; charity envieth not; charity vaunteth not itself, is not puffed up,

Doth not behave itself unseemly, seeketh not her own, is not easily provoked, thinketh no evil;

Rejoiceth not in iniquity, but rejoiceth in the truth;

Beareth all things, believeth all things, hopeth all things, endureth all things.

Charity never faileth: but whether there be prophecies,

they shall fail; whether there be tongues, they shall cease; whether there be knowledge, it shall vanish away.

For we know in part, and we prophesy in part.

But when that which is perfect is come, then that which is in part shall be done away.

When I was a child, I spake as a child, I understood as a child, I thought as a child: but when I became a man, I put away childish things.

For now we see through a glass, darkly; but then face to face: now I know in part; but then shall I know even as also I am known.

And now abideth faith, hope, charity, these three; but the greatest of these is charity.

St. Paul, I Corinthians 13:1–13 (AV)

A New Heaven and a New Earth

And I saw a new heaven and a new earth: for the first heaven and the first earth were passed away; and there was no more sea.

And I John saw the holy city, new Jerusalem, coming down from God out of heaven, prepared as a bride adorned for her husband.

And I heard a great voice out of heaven saying, Behold, the tabernacle of God is with men, and he will dwell with them, and they shall be his people, and God himself shall be with them, and be their God.

And God shall wipe away all tears from their eyes; and there shall be no more death, neither sorrow, nor crying, neither shall there be any more pain: for the former things are passed away.

And he that sat upon the throne said, Behold, I make all things new. And he said unto me, Write: for these words are true and faithful.

And he said unto me, It is done. I am Alpha and Omega, the beginning and the end. I will give unto him that is athirst of the fountain of the water of life freely.

Revelation 21:1–6 (AV)

All Eyes, All Light, All Face, All Glory, and All Spirit

The soul that, prepared by the Holy Spirit to be his seat and house, and found worthy to participate in his Light, is illuminated by the beauty of his ineffable glory, becomes all light, all face, all eyes; there is no part of her that is not full of these spiritual eyes of light. That is to say no part of her is in shadow, but she is entirely transformed into light and spirit and is all full of eyes and has neither a part behind or a part in front but appears all face because of the ineffable glory of the Light of Christ, that has descended on her and lives with her. And as the sun is totally of one likeness, and has no "behind" or imperfect part, but is throughout splendid with light, and is light throughout; or even as fire, that is to say the light of fire is entirely like itself and has no before or behind, greater or less; so too the soul that is perfectly illuminated by the ineffable glory of the light of the face of Christ, and perfectly partakes of the Holy Spirit, and is judged worthy to be made the house and seat of God, becomes all eyes, all light, all face, all glory and all spirit. . . .

If then you have become the throne of God, and the Heavenly Charioteer has seated himself within you, and your soul is entirely transformed into a spiritual eye, and is made into light; if you too are nourished with the heavenly food of that spirit and have drunk of the Living Water, and have put on the secret garment of light — if your inward being has experienced all these things and is established in rich unshakable faith, then you are living the Eternal Life, and your soul even in this present time rests with Christ.

Saint Macarius of Egypt

My Sins Are Running Out Behind Me

A brother in Scete committed a fault, the elders assembled, and sent for Abbot Moses to join them. He did not want to come. The priest sent him a message, saying: "Come, the community is waiting for you." So he arose and started off. He took with him a very old basket full of holes, filled it with sand, and carried it behind him. The elders came out to meet him, and said: "What is this, Father?" The elder replied: "My sins are running out behind me, and I do not see them, and today I come to judge the sins of another!" Hearing this, he said nothing to the brother and forgave him.

Sayings of the Desert Fathers

TO HIS LAST BREATH

The brethren asked Abba Agathon: "Amongst all our different activities, father, which is the virtue that requires the greatest effort?" He answered: "Forgive me, but I think there is no labor greater than praying to God. For every time a man wants to pray, his enemies the demons try to prevent him; for they know that nothing obstructs them so much as prayer to God. In everything else that a man undertakes, if he perseveres, he will attain rest. But in order to pray a man must struggle to his last breath."

Sayings of the Desert Fathers

Take Care of the Sick

A brother asked one of the elders, "There are two brothers, of whom one remains praying in his cell, fasting six days at a time and doing great penance. The other one takes care of the sick. Which one's work is more pleasing to God?" The elder replied: "If that brother who fasts six days at a time hanged himself up by the nose, he could not match the one who takes care of the sick."

Sayings of the Desert Fathers

Why Not Be Utterly Changed into Fire?

Abbot Lot came to Abbot Joseph and said: "Father, to the limit of my ability, I keep my little rule, my little fast, my prayer, meditation and contemplative silence; and to the limit of my ability, I work to cleanse my heart of thoughts; what more should I do?" The elder rose up in reply, and stretched out his hands to heaven, and his fingers became like ten lamps of fire. He said: "Why not be utterly changed into fire?"

Sayings of the Desert Fathers

Entering the Dark Cloud

But what now is the meaning of Moses' entry into the darkness and of the vision of God that he enjoyed in it? The present text (Exodus 24:15) would seem to be somewhat contradictory to the divine apparition he has seen before. There he saw God in the light, whereas he sees him in the darkness. But we should not therefore think that this contradicts the entire sequence of spiritual lessons that we have been considering. For the sacred text is here teaching us that spiritual knowledge first occurs as an illumination in those who experience it. Indeed, all that is opposed to piety is conceived of as darkness; to shun the darkness is to share in the light.

But as the soul makes progress, and by a greater and more perfect concentration comes to appreciate what the knowledge of truth is, the more it approaches this vision, and so much the more does it see that the divine nature is invisible. It thus leaves all surface appearances, not only those that can be grasped by the senses but also those that the mind itself seems to see, and it keeps on going deeper until by the operation of the spirit it penetrates the invisible and incomprehensible, and it is there that it sees God. The true vision and the true knowledge of what we seek consists precisely in not seeing, in an awareness that our goal transcends all knowledge and is everywhere cut off from us by the darkness of incomprehensibility. Thus that profound evangelist, John, who penetrated into this luminous darkness, tells us that no man hath seen God at any time (John 1:18), teaching us by this negation that no man — indeed, no created intellect — can attain knowledge of God.

Gregory of Nyssa

The Doctrine of Infinite Growth

The great Apostle told the Corinthians of the wonderful visions he enjoyed during the time of his mystical initiation in paradise. It was a time when he even doubted his own nature, whether he was body or spirit — and he testifies: *I do not count myself to have apprehended. But forgetting the things that are behind, I stretch myself forth to those that are before* (Philippians 3:13). And clearly this is meant to include even that third heaven that Paul alone saw; for even Moses told us nothing of it in his cosmogony. Yet even after listening in secret to the mysteries of heaven, Paul does not let the graces he has obtained become the limit of his desire, but he continues to go on and on, never ceasing his ascent. Thus he teaches us, I think, that in our constant participation in the blessed nature of the Good, the graces that we receive at every point are indeed great, but the path that lies beyond our immediate grasp is infinite. This will constantly happen to those who thus share in the divine Goodness, and they will always enjoy a greater and greater participation in grace throughout all eternity.

The pure of heart will see God, according to the Lord's infallible word (Matthew 5:8), according to his capacity, receiving as much as his mind can sustain; yet the infinite and incomprehensible nature of the Godhead remains beyond all understanding. For *the magnificence of his glory,* as the Prophet says, has no end, and as we contemplate him he remains ever the same, at the same distance above us. The great David enjoyed in his heart those glorious elevations as he progressed from strength to strength; and yet he cried to God: Lord, *thou art the most High,* forever and ever. And by this I think he means that in all the infinite eternity of centuries, the man who runs toward thee constantly becomes greater as he rises higher, ever growing in proportion to his increase in grace. *Thou,* indeed, *art the most High,* abiding forever, and canst never seem smaller to those who approach thee for thou art always to the same degree higher and loftier than the faculties of those who are rising.

This, then, is the doctrine that I think the Apostle is teaching about the ineffable nature of the Good, when he says that the eye does not know it even though it may see it. For the eye does not see it completely as it is, but only insofar as it can receive it. So too, even though we may constantly listen to the Word, we do not hear it completely according to its manifestation. And even though the clean of heart use his eyes as much as he can, yet it has not *entered into the heart of man*. Thus though the new grace we may obtain is greater than what we had before, it does not put a limit on our final goal; rather, for those who are rising in perfection, the limit of the good that is attained becomes the beginning of the discovery of higher goods. Thus they never stop rising, moving from one new beginning to the next, and the beginning of ever greater graces is never limited of itself. For the desire of those who thus rise never rests in what they can already understand; but by an ever greater and greater desire, the soul keeps rising constantly to another that lies ahead, and thus it makes its way through ever higher regions towards the Transcendent.

Gregory of Nyssa

UNITY IN DIVERSITY

All that the Father is, we see revealed in the Son; all that is the Son's is the Father's also; for the whole Son dwells in the Father, and he has the whole Father dwelling in himself. . . . The Son who exists always in the Father can never be separated from him, nor can the Spirit ever be divided from the Son who through the Spirit works all things. He who receives the Father also receives at the same time the Son and the Spirit. It is impossible to envisage any kind of severance or disjunction between them: One cannot think of the Son apart from the Father, nor divide the Spirit from the Son. There is between the three a sharing and a differentiation that are beyond words and understanding.

The distinction between the persons does not impair the oneness of nature, nor does the shared unity of essence lead to a confusion between the distinctive characteristics of the persons. Do not be surprised that we should speak of the Godhead as being at the same time both unified and differentiated. Using riddles, as it were, we envisage a strange and paradoxical diversity-in-unity and unity-in-diversity.

Gregory of Nyssa

The Radiance of
the Divine Darkness

Trinity!! Higher than any being,
   any divinity, any goodness!
Guide of Christians
   in the wisdom of heaven!
Lead us up beyond unknowing and light,
   up to the farthest, highest peak
   of mystic scripture,
where the mysteries of God's Word
   lie simple, absolute and unchangeable
   in the brilliant darkness of a hidden silence.
Amid the deepest shadow
   they pour overwhelming light
   on what is most manifest.
Amid the wholly unsensed and unseen
   they completely fill our sightless minds
With treasures beyond all beauty.

Leave the senses and the workings of the intellect, and all
that the sense and the intellect can perceive, and all that is

50

not and that is; and through unknowing reach out, so far as this is possible, toward oneness with him who is beyond all being and knowledge. In this way, through an uncompromising, absolute, and pure detachment from yourself and from all things, transcending all things and released from all, you will be led upwards toward that radiance of the divine darkness that is beyond all being.

Entering the darkness that surpasses understanding, we shall find ourselves brought, not just to brevity of speech, but to perfect silence and unknowing.

Emptied of all knowledge, man is joined in the highest part of himself, not with any created thing, nor with himself, nor with another, but with the One who is altogether unknowable; and in knowing nothing, he knows in a manner that surpasses understanding.

Dionysius the Areopagite

ENTERING INTO JOY

Imagine if all the tumult of the body were to quiet down, along with all our busy thoughts about earth, sea, and air; if the very world should stop, and the mind cease thinking about itself, go beyond itself, and be quite still; if all the fantasies that appear in dreams and imagination should cease, and there be no speech, no sign: Imagine if all things that are perishable grew still — for if we listen they are saying, "We did not make ourselves; he made us who abides forever" — imagine, then, that they should say this and fall silent, listening to the very voice of him who made them and not to that of his creation; so that we should hear not his word through the tongues of men, nor the voice of angels, nor the clouds' thunder, nor any symbol, but the very Self which in these things we love, and go beyond ourselves to attain a flash of that eternal wisdom that abides above all things: And imagine if that moment were to go on and on, leaving behind all other sights and sounds but this one vision that ravishes and absorbs and fixes the beholder in joy; so that the rest of eternal life were like that moment of illumination that leaves us breathless:

Would this not be what is bidden in scripture, Enter thou into the joy of thy Lord?

Saint Augustine

SHE LEADS US ALL
TO DIVINE KNOWLEDGE

We see the Holy Virgin as a flaming torch appearing to those in darkness. For having kindled the Immaterial Light, she leads all to divine knowledge; she illumines our minds with radiance and is honored by our shouting these praises:

Rejoice, ray of the spiritual Sun!

Rejoice, flash of unfading splendour!

Rejoice, lightning that lights up our souls!

Rejoice, thunder that stuns our enemies!

Rejoice, for you caused the refulgent Light to dawn!

Rejoice, for you caused the river of many streams to gush forth!

Rejoice, living image of the font!

Rejoice, remover of the stain of sin!

Rejoice, laver that washes the conscience clean!

Rejoice, bowl for mixing the wine of joy!

Rejoice, aroma of the fragrance of Christ!

Rejoice, life of mystical festivity!
Rejoice, unwedded Bride!

Eikos 2 from the *A*kathist Hymn of
Romanus the Melodist

HEALING OF MY BODY
AND SALVATION OF MY SOUL

While singing to thy Child, we all praise you as a living temple, O Mother of God. For the Lord who holds all things in his hand dwelt in thy womb, and he sanctified and glorified you, and taught all to cry to you:

Rejoice, tabernacle of God the Word!

Rejoice, saint greater than the saints!

Rejoice, ark made golden by the Spirit!

Rejoice, inexhaustible treasury of Life!

Rejoice, precious diadem of pious kings!

Rejoice, beloved boast of devoted priests!

Rejoice, unshaken tower of the Church!

Rejoice, impregnable wall of the Kingdom!

Rejoice, thou through whom we obtain our victories!

Rejoice, thou before whom our foes fall prostrate!

Rejoice, healing of my body!

Rejoice, salvation of my soul!

Rejoice, unwedded Bride!

Eikos 12 from the Akathist Hymn of
Romanus the Melodist

An Invocation to the Holy Spirit

Come, true light.

Come, life eternal.

Come, hidden mystery.

Come, treasure without name.

Come, reality beyond all words.

Come, person beyond all understanding.

Come, rejoicing without end.

Come, light that knows no evening.

Come, unfailing expectation of the saved.

Come, raising of the fallen.

Come, resurrection of the dead.

Come all-powerful, for unceasingly you create, refashion and change all things by your will alone.

Come, invisible whom none may touch and handle.

Come, for you continue always unmoved, yet at every instant you are wholly in movement; you draw near to us who lie in hell, yet you remain higher than the heavens.

Come, for your name fills our hearts with longing and is

ever on our lips; yet who you are and what your nature
is, we cannot say or know.

Come, Alone to the alone.

Come, for you are yourself the desire that is within me.

Come, my breath and my life.

Come, the consolation of my humble soul.

Come, my joy, my glory, my endless delight.

Saint Symeon the New Theologian

Beyond Nature, Thought, or Conception

That human being who is inwardly illumined by the light of the Holy Spirit cannot endure the vision of it, but falls face down on the ground and cries out in great fear and wonder, because he has seen and experienced something that is beyond nature, thought, or conception. He becomes like someone suddenly inflamed with a violent fever; as though on fire and powerless to control the flames, he is beside himself, totally incapable of controlling himself. And though he weeps incessant tears that bring some relief, the flame of his desire breaks out even more intensely. Then his tears flow even more abundantly and washed by their flow, he becomes even more radiant. When, utterly incandescent, he has become like light, then the saying of Saint Gregory of Nazianzos is fulfilled, "God is united with gods and known by them," in the sense perhaps that he is now united to those who have joined themselves to him, and revealed to those who have come to know him.

Saint Symeon the New Theologian

Guard the Heart

True and unerring attentiveness mean that the intellect keeps watch over the heart while it prays. It should always be on patrol within the heart, and from within — from the depths of the heart — it should offer up its prayers to God. Our holy fathers listened to the Lord's words, "Out of the heart proceed evil thoughts, murders, adulteries, unchastity, thefts, perjuries, blasphemies: these are the things that defile a man" (Matthew 15:19–20) and they listened to him when he told us to clean the inside of the cup so that the outside may also be clean (Matthew 23:26). This is why they abandoned all other forms of spiritual labor and concentrated completely on this one task of guarding the heart, convinced that through this practice they would also come to possess every other virtue, while without it no virtue could be firmly established.

Saint Symeon the New Theologian

Take the Poor Man In

Our Lord was pleased to assume the likeness of every poor man and compared himself to every poor man in order that no man who believes in him should exalt himself over his brother, but, seeing his Lord in his brother, should consider himself less and worse than his brother, just as he is less than his Creator, and should take the poor man in and honor him, and be ready to exhaust all his means in helping him, just as our Lord Jesus Christ exhausted his blood for our salvation.

Saint Symeon the New Theologian

A Charitable Heart

What is a charitable heart? It is a heart that is burning with charity for the whole of creation, for men, for the birds, for the beasts, for the demons — for all creatures. He who has such a heart cannot see or call to mind a creature without his eyes becoming filled with tears by reason of the immense compassion that seizes his heart, a heart that is softened and can no longer bear to see or learn from others of any suffering, even the smallest pain, being inflicted upon a creature. This is why such a man never ceases to pray also for the animals, for the enemies of Truth, and for those who do him evil, that they may be preserved and purified. He will pray even for the reptiles, moved by the infinite pity that reigns in the hearts of those who are becoming united to God.

Saint Isaac the Syrian

Constant Prayer

When a man has been granted constant prayer, it will mean that he has reached the summit of all virtues and has become the abode of the Holy Spirit; for a man who has not wholly received this grace of the Comforter cannot keep this prayer in his heart with joy. Therefore it is said that when the Holy Spirit comes to live in a man, he never ceases to pray, for then the Holy Spirit himself constantly prays in him (Romans 8:26). Then prayer never stops in a man's soul, whether he is asleep or awake. In eating or drinking, sleeping or doing something, even in deep sleep his heart sends forth without effort the incense and sighs of prayer. Then prayer never leaves him, but at every hour, even if externally silent, it continues secretly to act within. This is why someone has called the silence of the pure bearers of Christ — prayer; for their thoughts are Divine movements, and the movements of mind and heart that are pure are meek voices by which they secretly sing praises to the One who is in secret.

Saint Isaac the Syrian

HOW BEST TO SAY THE JESUS PRAYER

You know that our breathing is the inhaling and exhaling of air. The organ that serves for this is the lungs that lie round the heart, so that the air passing through them thereby envelops the heart. Thus breathing is a natural way to the heart. And so, having collected your mind within you, lead it into the channel of breathing through which air reaches the heart and, together with this inhaled air, force your mind to descend into the heart and to remain there. Accustom it not to come out of the heart too soon, for at first it feels very lonely in that inner seclusion and imprisonment. But when it gets accustomed to it, it begins on the contrary to dislike its aimless circling outside, for it is no longer unpleasant and wearisome for it to be within. Just as a man who has been away from home, when he returns is beside himself with joy at seeing again his children and wife, embraces them and cannot talk to them enough, so the mind, when it unites with the heart, is filled with unspeakable joy and delight. Then a man sees that the Kingdom of Heaven is truly within us; and seeing it now in himself, he strives with pure prayer to keep it and strengthen it there.

When you thus enter into the place of the heart, as I have shown you, give thanks to God and, praising his mercy, keep always to this doing, and it will teach you things that in no other way you will ever learn. Moreover you should know that when your mind becomes firmly established in the heart, it must not remain there silent and idle, but it should constantly repeat the Jesus prayer: "Lord, Jesus Christ, Son of God, have mercy upon me!" and never cease. For this practice, keeping the mind from dreams, renders it elusive and impenetrable to enemy suggestions and every day leads it more and more to love and longing for God.

Nicephorus the Solitary

And the Faithful
Shall Abide with Him

Truly blessed is he who cleaves with his thought to the Prayer of Jesus, constantly calling to him in his heart, just as air cleaves to our bodies or the flame to the candle. The sun, passing over the earth, produces daylight; the holy and worshipful Name of Lord Jesus, constantly shining in the mind, produces a measureless number of sun-like thoughts.

When the clouds disperse, the air appears pure. When passionate fantasies are dispersed by the Sun of Truth, Jesus Christ, radiant and star-like thoughts are naturally born in the heart, for Jesus illumines the air of the heart with his light. The wise Solomon says: "They that put their trust in him shall understand the truth; and such as be faithful in love shall abide with him" (Wisdom of Solomon 3:9).

Hesychius of Jerusalem

GOD'S WORD IS IN ALL CREATION

No creature has meaning without the Word of God.
God's Word is in all creation, visible and invisible.
The Word is living, being, spirit, all verdant greening,
    all creativity.
This Word flashes out in every creature.
This is how the spirit is in the flesh — the Word is
    indivisible from God.

Hildegard of Bingen

To the Virgin

O greening branch
You stand in your nobility
Like the rising dawn
Rejoice now and exult
And deign to free the fools we are
From our long slavery to evil
And hold out your hand
To raise us up.

Hildegard of Bingen

On the Assumption

The glorious Virgin has ascended into heaven. . . . If the soul of an unborn child melted in bliss when Mary spoke, what was the joy of the citizens of heaven when they not only heard her voice but saw her face and reveled in her blessed presence among them? The whole universe is lit up by the presence of Mary, so much so that even heaven itself, irradiated with the light of her virginal brightness, takes on a new brilliance. Rightly then do praise and thanksgiving resound on high, but it might seem more fitting for us to cry rather than clap our hands! If heaven rejoices in Mary's presence, does it not follow that our world below should proportionately mourn her absence?

But let that be the end of our grieving, for here we have no abiding city: We seek the very city to which blessed Mary has gone. If we are enrolled as citizens of heaven, it is surely right for us to remember her and to share her happiness even in our exile, even here beside the waters of Babylon. Our queen has gone before us, and so glorious has been her entry into paradise that we, her slaves, confidently follow our mistress, crying: *Draw us after you and we shall run in the fragrance of your perfumes.* As mother of our judge and mother of mercy, she will humbly and effectively handle the affairs of our salvation.

Earth has sent a priceless gift up to heaven, so that by giving and receiving within the blessed bond of friendship, the human wedded to the divine, earth to heaven, the depths to the heights.

Saint Bernard of Clairvaux

Mary, Star of the Sea

O you, whoever you are, who feel that in the tidal wave of this world you are nearer to being tossed about among the squalls and gales than treading on dry land, if you do not want to founder in the tempest, do not avert your eyes from the brightness of this star. When the wind of temptation blows up within you, when you strike upon the rock of tribulation, gaze up at this star, call out to Mary. Whether you are being tossed about by the waves of pride or ambition or slander or jealousy, gaze up at this star, call out to Mary. When rage or greed or fleshly desires are battering the skiff of your soul, gaze up at Mary. When the immensity of your sins weighs you down and you are bewildered by the loathsomeness of your conscience, when the terrifying thought of judgment appalls you and you begin to founder in the gulf of sadness and despair, think of Mary. In dangers, in hardships, in every doubt, think of Mary, call out to Mary. Keep her in your mouth, keep her in your heart. Follow the example of her life and you will obtain the favor of her prayer. Following her, you will never go astray. Asking her help, you will never despair. Keeping her in your thoughts, you will never wander away. With your hand in hers, you will never stumble. With her protecting you, you will not be afraid. With her leading you, you will never tire. Her kindness will see you through to the end.

Saint Bernard of Clairvaux

The Four Degrees
of Passionate Charity

The first degree of passionate charity is love that wounds; the second is love that binds. Love rises up to the third degree of passion, when it excludes every other love, but the one, for the sake of the one. The fourth degree of passionate love is that in which nothing at all can satisfy the desire of the passionate soul.

The first degree of violence in the passion of love is when the mind cannot resist its desires; the second when it cannot forget them; the third when nothing else can please it; the fourth and last when even this love cannot satisfy it. In the first love is insuperable; in the second inseparable; in the third singular; in the fourth insatiable. Love is insuperable when it will not yield to any other feeling; inseparable when it never leaves the memory; singular when it will have no companion; insatiable when it cannot be satisfied.

Let us speak more deeply and openly. In the first degree the soul thirsts for God; in the second she thirsts to go to God; in the third she thirsts to be in God; in the fourth she thirsts in God's way. She thirsts for God when she desires to experience what that inward sweetness is that makes drunk the mind of man, when he begins to taste and see how sweet the Lord is. She thirsts to go to God when she desires to be raised above herself by the grace of contemplation and to see the Lord in all his beauty. . . . She thirsts in God when she desires to pass over into God altogether. . . . She thirsts in God's way, when, by her own will I do not mean in temporal matters only but also in spiritual things, the soul reserves nothing for her own will but commits all things to God, never thinking about herself but about the things of Jesus Christ, so that she may say "I came not to do my own will but to do the will of my Father in heaven." In the first degree God enters into the soul and she turns inward into herself. In the second she ascends above herself and is lifted up to God. In the third the soul, lifted up to God, passes over completely into him. In the fourth the soul goes forth on God's behalf and descends below herself.

The first degree of violent love wounds the affection; the second binds the thoughts; the third hinders action. When in this way the soul has been reduced in the divine fire, softened to the very core and entirely melted, nothing is wanting except that she should be shown what is God's goodwill, all-pleasing and perfect, even the form of perfect virtue to which she must be conformed. Just as metal workers, when the metals are melted and the molds set out, shape any form according to their will and produce any vessel according to the manner and mold that has been planned, so the soul applies herself in this degree, to be ready at the summons of the divine will; she adapts herself with spontaneous desire to every demand of God and adjusts her own will, as the divine pleasure requires. And as liquefied metal runs down slowly wherever a passage is opened, so the soul humbles herself spontaneously to be obedient in this way, and freely bows herself in all acts of humility according to the order of divine providence. In this state the image of the will of Christ is set before the soul so that these words come to her: "Let this mind be in you, which is also in Christ Jesus, who being in the form of God, thought it not robbery to be equal with God, but emptied himself, and took upon himself the form of a servant and was made in the likeness of man. He humbled himself and became obedient unto death, even the death of the Cross." This is the form of the humility of Christ to which every man must conform himself, who longs to attain to the highest degree of charity. For greater love has no man than this, that a man lay down his life for his friends. Those who are able to lay down their lives for their friends have reached the highest peak of charity. . . . They can answer to the Apostle's call: "Be you therefore followers of God, as dear children: and walk in love, as

Christ has also loved us, and has given himself for an offering to God for a fragrant saviour." Therefore, in the third degree the soul is glorified; in the fourth she is humbled for God's sake. In the third she is conformed to the divine light; in the fourth she is conformed to the humility of Christ. And though in the third she is in a way almost in the likeness of God, nevertheless in the fourth she starts to empty herself, taking the form of a servant. In the third degree of passionate charity the soul is, as it were, put to death in God; in the fourth she is raised in Christ. He that is in the fourth degree can truly say: "I live yet not I, Christ liveth in me." He who ascends to this degree of charity is truly in the state of love that can say: "I am made all things to all men that I might save all." ... That which he hopes of God, what he does for God and in God and effects with God is more than merely human.

Richard of Saint Victor
Adapted from the translation of
Clare Kirchberger

Lord, Make Me an Instrument of Thy Peace

Lord, make me an instrument of thy peace.
Where there is hatred, let me sow love;
Where there is injury, pardon;
Where there is doubt, faith;
Where there is despair, hope;
Where there is darkness, light;
Where there is sadness, joy.
O divine Master, grant that I may not so much seek
To be consoled as to console,
To be understood as to understand,
To be loved as to love;
For it is in giving that we receive;
It is in pardoning that we are pardoned;
It is in dying to self that we are born to eternal life.

Saint Francis of Assisi

The Song of the Sun

All Glory to you, most high, omnipotent, and good Lord
Praise and honor forever, and every blessing.
To you alone, most high One, should these be given
And no man is worthy of naming you.
Glory to you, my Lord, for all your creatures
Especially our brother, the sun,
Who is the day, and by whom you give us light:
He is beautiful and radiant with great splendor
And bears witness to you, most high One.
Glory to you, my Lord, for sister moon and the stars
You have made in heaven clear, precious, and beautiful.
Glory to you, my Lord, for brother wind
And for air and cloud and serene sky
And all the different weathers
By which you sustain all creatures.
Glory to you, my Lord, for sister water
Who is very useful and humble
And precious and pure.
Glory to you, my Lord, for brother fire
By whom you illumine night

And he is beautiful and joyful and robust and full of
    power.
Glory to you, my Lord, for our sister mother earth
Who sustains and governs us
And produces different fruits
And brightly colored flowers and grass.
Glory to you, my Lord,
For those who forgive for love of you
And bear sickness and ordeals.
Happy are those who bear them in peace
For they will be crowned by you, most high Lord.
Glory be to you, my Lord,
For our sister bodily death
From whom no living man can escape.
Grief to all those who die
In mortal sin —
Happy those whom death will find
Firm in your holy will —
The second death will do them no harm.
Praise and bless my Lord
Be grateful to him,
And serve him in great humility.

Saint Francis of Assisi

How the Soul through the Senses Finds God in All Creatures

O Love, divine Love, why do you lay siege to me?
In a frenzy of love for me, you find no rest.

From five sides you move against me,
Hearing, sight, taste, touch, and scent.
To come out is to be caught; I cannot hide from you.

If I come through sight I see Love
Painted in every form and color,
Inviting me to come to you, to dwell in you.

If I leave through the door of hearing,
What I hear points only to you, Lord;
I cannot escape Love through this gate.

If I come out through taste, every flavor proclaims:
"Love, divine Love, hungering Love!
You have caught me on your hook, for you want to reign
    in me."

If I leave through the door of scent
I sense you in all creation; you have caught me
And wounded me through that fragrance.

If I come out through the sense of touch
I find your lineaments in every creature;
To try to flee from you is madness.

Love, I flee from you, afraid to give you my heart:
I see that you make me one with you,
I cease to be me and can no longer find myself.

If I see evil in a man or defect or temptation,
You fuse me with him, and make me suffer;
O Love without limits, who is it you love?

It is you, O Crucified Christ,
Who takes possession of me,
Drawing me out of the sea to the shore;

There I suffer to see your wounded heart.
Why did you endure the pain?
So that I might be healed.

Jacopone da Todi

God Speaks to the Soul

And God said to the soul:
I desired you before the world began.
I desire you now
As you desire me.
And where the desires of two come together
There love is perfected.

How the Soul Speaks to God
Lord, you are my lover,
My longing,
My flowing stream,
My sun,
And I am your reflection.

How God Answers the Soul
It is my nature that makes me love you often,
For I am love itself.
It is my longing that makes me love you intensely,

For I yearn to be loved from the heart.
It is my eternity that makes me love you long,
For I have no end.

Mechthild of Magdeburg

To Live Out What I Am

My distress is great and unknown to men.
They are cruel to me, for they wish to dissuade me
From all that the forces of Love urge me to.
They do not understand it, and I cannot explain it to
   them.
 I must then live out what I am;
 What Love counsels my spirit,
In this is my being: for this reason I will do my best.

Whatever vicissitudes men lead me through for Love's
   sake,
I wish to stand firm and take no harm from them.
For I understand from the nobility of my soul
That in suffering for sublime Love, I conquer.
 I will therefore gladly surrender myself
 In pain, in repose, in dying, in living,
For I know the command of lofty fidelity.

I do not complain of suffering for Love:
It becomes me always to submit to her,

Whether she commands in storm or in stillness.
One can know her only in herself.
This is an unconceivable wonder,
Which has thus filled my heart
And makes me stray in a wild desert.

Hadewijch of Antwerp

Subject to That Great Power

What satisfies Love best of all is that we be wholly stripped of all repose, whether in strangers, or in friends, or even in Love herself. And this is a frightening life Love wants, that we must do without the satisfaction of Love in order to satisfy Love. They who are thus drawn and accepted by Love, and fettered by her, are the most indebted to Love, and consequently they must continually stand subject to the great power of her strong nature, to content her. And that life is miserable beyond all that the human heart can bear.

For nothing in their life satisfies them — either their gifts, or their service, or consolations, or all they can accomplish. For interiorly Love draws them so strongly to her, and they feel Love so vast and so incomprehensible; and they find themselves too small for this, and too inadequate to satisfy that Essence which is Love. And they are aware that they themselves owe such a heavy debt, which they must pay by contenting Love in all manners, that with relation to everything else they can experience neither pleasure nor pain, either in themselves or in other people, except where Love herself is concerned. Only in this case could they experience pleasure or pain: pleasure, in proportion as Love was advanced or grew in themselves and in others; pain, in proportion as Love was hindered or harmed in those who love.

Hadewijch of Antwerp

Behold My Humility

The eyes of my soul were opened, and I beheld the pleni-
tude of God, wherein I did comprehend the whole world,
both here and beyond the sea, and the abyss and ocean
and all things. In all these things I beheld naught save the
divine power, in a manner assuredly indescribable; so that
through excess of marveling the soul cried with a loud
voice, saying, "This whole world is full of God!" Wherefore
I now comprehended how small a thing is the whole
world, that is to say both here and beyond the seas, the
abyss, the ocean, and all things; and that the Power of God
exceeds and fills all. Then he said unto me: "I have shown
thee something of my Power," and I understood, that after
this I should better understand the rest. He then said,
"Behold now my humility." Then I was given an insight
into the deep humility of God toward man. And compre-
hending that unspeakable power and beholding that deep
humility, my soul marveled greatly, and did esteem itself
to be nothing at all.

Angela of Foligno

Seeing God in and with Darkness

Christ's faithful one said the following: Once my soul was elevated, and I saw the light, the beauty, and the fullness that is in God in a way that I had never seen before in so great a manner. I did not see love there. I then lost the love which was mine and was made nonlove.

Afterward, I saw him in a darkness, and in a darkness precisely because the good that he is, is far too great to be conceived or understood. Indeed, anything conceivable or understandable does not attain this good or even come near it. My soul was then granted a most certain faith, a secure and most firm hope, a continual security about God that took away all my fear. In this good, which is seen in the darkness, I recollected myself totally. I was made so sure of God that in no way can I ever entertain any doubts about him or of my possession of him. Of this I have the utmost certitude. And in this most efficacious good seen in this darkness now resides my most firm hope, one in which I am totally recollected and secure. . . .

As I, brother scribe, resisted what she said about this darkness and did not understand her, Christ's faithful one told me by way of explanation: The All Good was all the more certain and superior to everything the more it was seen in darkness and most secret. This is why I see the All Good accompanied with darkness: because it surpasses every good. All else, in comparison, is but darkness. No matter how far the soul or heart expands itself, all that expanse is less than this good. What I related until now — that is, when the soul sees all creation overflowing with God's presence, when it sees the divine power or the divine wisdom — all this is inferior to this most secret good, because this good which I see with darkness is the whole, and all other things are but parts. . . .

When God is seen in darkness it does not bring a smile to the lips, nor devotion, fervor, or ardent love; neither does the body or the soul tremble or move as at other times; the soul sees nothing and everything; the body sleeps and speech is cut off. God spoke to me, all those which you ever wrote — I now understand that these were so much less than that which I see with such great darkness, that in no way do I place my hope in them, nor is there any of my hope in them. Even if it were possible that all these previous experiences were not true, nonetheless, that could in no way diminish my hope — the hope that is so secure and certain in the All Good which I see with such darkness. Christ's faithful one told me, that her soul had been elevated only three times to this most exalted and altogether ineffable way of seeing God with such darkness, a vision which was a superlative and utterly wonderful grace. . . . "For in this state it seems to me that I am standing or lying in the midst of the Trinity."

Angela of Foligno

The Divine Birth

God gives birth to the Son as you, as me, as each one of us. As many beings — as many gods in God. In my soul, God not only gives birth to me as his son, he gives birth to me as himself, and himself as me.

I find in this divine birth that God and I are the same: I am what I was and what I shall always remain, now and forever. I am transported above the highest angels; I neither decrease nor increase, for in this birth I have become the motionless cause of all that moves. I have won back what has always been mine. Here, in my own soul, the greatest of all miracles has taken place — God has returned to God!

Meister Eckhart

THE SPARK AND THE GROUND

Therefore, I say, if a man turns away from self and from created things, then — to the extent that you do this — you will attain oneness and blessedness in your soul's spark, which time and place never touched. This spark is opposed to all creatures, it wants nothing but God naked, just as he is. It is not satisfied with the Father, or the Son, or the Holy Ghost, or all three Persons so far as they preserve their several properties. I declare in truth, this light would not be satisfied with the unity of the whole fertility of the divine nature. In fact I will say still more, which sounds even stranger: I declare on all truth, by the eternal and everlasting truth, that this light is not content with the simple, changeless divine being that neither gives nor takes; rather it seeks to know whence this being comes, it wants to get into its simple Ground, into the Silent Desert, into which no distinction ever peeped of Father, Son or Holy Ghost.

Meister Eckhart

Sermon Nineteen

Surrexit Autem Saulus De Terra Apertisque Oculis Nihil Videbat

This text which I have quoted in Latin is written by Saint Luke in Acts about Saint Paul. It means: "Paul rose from the ground and with open eyes saw nothing."

I think this text has a fourfold sense. One is that when he rose up from the ground with open eyes he saw Nothing, and the Nothing was God; for when he saw God he calls that Nothing. The second: When he got up he saw nothing but God. The third: In all things he saw nothing but God. The fourth: When he saw God, he saw all things as nothing. . . .

"Paul rose from the ground and with open eyes saw nothing.". . .

A master says whoever speaks of God in any likeness, speaks impurely of him. But to speak of God with nothing is to speak of him correctly. When the soul is unified and there enters into total self-abnegation, then she finds God as in Nothing. It appeared to a man as in a dream — it was a waking dream — that he became pregnant with Nothing like a woman with child, and in that Nothing God was born; he was the fruit of nothing. God was born in the Nothing. . . .

If we are to know God it must be without means, and then nothing alien can enter in. If we do see God in this light, it must be quite private and indrawn, without the intrusion of anything created. Then we have an immediate knowledge of eternal life. . . .

For God to be perceived by the soul, she must be blind. Therefore, he says, "He saw the Nothing," from whose light all lights come, from whose essence all essence comes. And so the bride says in the Book of Love: "When I had passed on a little further, I found him that my soul loves." The little that she passed by was all creatures. Whoever does not put them behind him will not find God. She also means that however subtle, however pure a thing is that I know God by, yet it must go. Even the light that is truly God, if I take it where it touches my soul, that is still not right. I must take it there, where it wells forth. I could not properly see the light that shines on the wall unless I turned my gaze to where it comes from. And even then, if I take it where it wells forth, I must be free of this welling forth: I must take it where it rests in itself, for these are still all modes. We must take God as mode without mode, and essence without essence, for he has no modes. Therefore Saint Bernard says, "He who would know thee, God, must measure thee without measure."

Let us pray to our Lord that we may come to that understanding that is wholly without mode and without measure.

Meister Eckhart

Vision of God

O grace abounding that had made me fit
to fix my eyes on the eternal light
until my vision was consumed in it!

I saw within its depth how it conceives
all things in a single volume bound by Love,
of which the universe is the scattered leaves;

substance, accident, and their relation
so fused that all I say could do no more
than yield a glimpse of that bright revelation.

I think I saw the universal form
that binds these things, for as I speak these words
I feel my joy swell and my spirits warm.

Twenty-five centuries since Neptune saw
the Argo's keel have not moved all mankind,
recalling that adventure, to such awe

as I felt in an instant. My tranced being
stared fixed and motionless upon that vision,
ever more fervent to see in the act of seeing.

Experiencing that Radiance, the spirit
is so indrawn it is impossible
even to think of ever turning from it.

For the good which is the will's ultimate object
is all subsumed in it; and, being removed,
all is defective which in it is perfect.

Now in my recollection of the rest
I have less power to speak than any infant
wetting its tongue yet at its mother's breast;

and not because that Living Radiance bore
more than one semblance, for it is unchanging
and is forever as it was before;

rather, as I grew worthier to see,
the more I looked, the more unchanging semblance
appeared to change with every change in me.

Within the depthless deep and clear existence
of that abyss of light three circles shown —
three in color, one in circumference:

the second from the first, rainbow from rainbow;
the third, an exhalation of pure fire
equally breathed forth by the other two.

But O how much my words miss my conception,
which is itself so far from what I saw
that to call it feeble would be rank deception!

O Light Eternal fixed in itself alone,
by itself alone understood, which from itself
loves and glows, self-knowing and self-known;

that second aureole which shone forth in Thee,
conceived as a reflection of the first —
or which appeared so to my scrutiny —

seemed in itself of its own coloration
to be painted with man's image. I fixed my eyes
on that alone in rapturous contemplation.

Like a geometer wholly dedicated
to squaring the circle, but who cannot find,
think as he may, the principle indicated —

so did I study the supernal face.
I yearned to know just how our image merges
into that circle, and how it here finds place;

but mine were not the wings for such a flight.
Yet, as I wished, the truth I wished for came
cleaving my mind in a great flash of light.

Here my powers rest from their high fantasy,
but already I could feel my being turned —
instinct and intellect balanced equally

as in a wheel whose motion nothing jars —
by the Love that moves the Sun and the other stars.

Dante Alighieri, *Paradiso*, canto 33

The Path of Pain

A man once thought that God drew some men even by pleasant paths, while other were drawn by the path of pain. Our Lord answered him thus, "What think ye can be pleasanter or nobler than to be made most like unto me? that is by suffering. Mark, to whom was ever offered such a troubled life as to me? And in whom can I better work in accordance with my true nobility than in those who are most like me? They are the men who suffer.... Learn that my divine nature never worked so nobly in human nature as by suffering; and because suffering is so effective, it is sent out of great love. I understand the weakness of human nature at all times, and out of love and righteousness I lay no heavier load on man than he can bear. The crown must be firmly pressed down that is to bud and blossom in the Eternal Presence of my Heavenly Father. He who desires to be wholly immersed in the fathomless sea of my Godhead must also be deeply immersed in the deep sea of bitter sorrow. I am exalted far above all things, and work supernaturally and wonderful works in myself:

The deeper and more supernaturally a man crushes himself beneath all things, the more supernaturally will he be drawn far above all things.

Johann Tauler

My Sufferings Are the Door

"None can come to the sublime heights of the divinity," said the Eternal Wisdom, "or taste its ineffable sweetness, if first they have not experienced the bitterness and lowliness of my humanity. The higher they climb without passing by my humanity, the lower afterward shall be their fall. My humanity is the road which all must tread who would come to that which you seek: my sufferings are the door by which all must come in."

Heinrich Suso

How Steadfastly One Must Fight Who Would Attain the Spiritual Prize

It was the intention and sincere wish of the servant to be found pleasing in God's eyes in an especially noble way, but without suffering or hard work. It once happened that he went out preaching across the land. And he got on board a public boat on the Lake of Constance where there sat among others an imposing young knight wearing courtly attire. He went over to the squire and asked him whose vassal he was. He answered, "I go forth on quests and gather the lords together for courtly activities. There they engage in swordplay and tournaments and serve beautiful ladies. Whoever succeeds in this the best is given honor and is rewarded." He asked, "What is the reward?" The knight said, "The most beautiful lady present puts a gold ring on his hand." Then he asked, "Tell me, dear sir, what does one have to do to attain the honor and the ring?" He said, "The one who suffers the most blows and sallies and does not falter but rather displays boldness and manliness, who sits firmly (in the saddle) and lets the blows rain on him — he receives the prize." He then asked, "Now tell me: If someone were bold during the first encounter, would that be enough?" He said, "No, he has to stand firm through the whole tournament, even if he is struck so that fire shoots out of his eyes and blood pours out of his mouth and nose. All this he must endure if he is to win praise." He asked further, "Dear friend, does he dare weep or act sad when he is so severely struck?" He answered, "No, even if his heart sinks within him, as happens to many, he can do nothing of the kind but must act as though nothing were wrong. He must act in a cheerful and elegant manner; otherwise, he would be mocked and would lose honor and the ring."

The servant was deeply affected within himself by this conversation. Sighing from the heart within him he said, "Noble sir, if the knights of this world have to take such sufferings upon themselves for so small a reward, which is nothing in itself, dear God, how just it then is that one must suffer many more trials for the eternal prize! O gentle Lord, if only I were worthy of becoming your spiritual knight. Beautiful, comely eternal Wisdom, whose riches of grace find no equal in all the lands, if only my soul could receive a ring from you! Indeed, for that I would be willing to suffer whatever you wanted." And he began to weep because of the intense emotion that had come over him.

When he came to the town that was his destination,

God visited him with so much serious suffering visible to all that the poor man almost gave up on God, and many an eye was wet out of pity for him. He forgot all about venturesome knighthood and the promises he made to God in his resolve about spiritual knighthood. He became sad and irritable with God, asking what he was blaming him for and why he was sending him such suffering. When the next morning arrived, calm entered his soul and with his senses withdrawn something spoke thus within him: "How is it now with your outstanding knightly endeavors? What good is a knight of straw and a man made of cloth? Great daring in good times and then giving up in bad times — no one has ever won the ring you long for that way." He answered and said, "O Lord, the tournaments that one has to endure for you are much too long and difficult." He received the answer: "But the praise, honor and ring of the knights that are honored by me are constant and last forever."

Heinrich Suso

Jesus, Are You Not My Mother?

Jesus, are you not my Mother? Are you not even more than my mother? My human mother after all laboured in giving birth to me for only a day or a night; You, my tender and beautiful Lord, laboured for me for over thirty years. ... Oh with what measureless love you laboured for me! ... But when the time was ripe for you to be delivered, your labor pains were so terrible your holy sweat was like great drops of blood that ran from your body onto the earth. ... Who ever saw a mother endure so dreadful a birth? When the time of your delivery came, you were nailed to the hard bed of the Cross . . . and your nerves and all your veins were broken. How could anyone be surprised that your veins broke open when in one day you gave birth to the whole world?

Marguerite of Oingt

Christ the Mother

I say that he is to us everything that is good and comforting for our help. He is our clothing, who wraps and enfolds us for love, embraces us and shelters us, surrounds us for his love, which is so tender that he may never desert us. . . . And in this he showed me something small, no bigger than a hazelnut, lying in the palm of my hand, as it seemed to me, and it was as round as a ball. I looked at it with the eye of my understanding and thought: What can this be? I was amazed that it could last, for I thought that because of its littleness it would suddenly have fallen into nothing. And I was answered in my understanding: It lasts and always will, because God loves it; and thus everything has being through the love of God. . . .

Our Mother in nature, or Mother in grace, because he wanted altogether to become our Mother in all things, made the foundation of his work most humbly and most mildly in the maiden's womb. . . . The mother's service is nearest, readiest, and surest: Nearest because it is most natural; readiest because it is most loving; and surest because it is truest. No one ever might or could perform this office fully, except only for him. We know that all our mothers bear us for pain and for death. O, what is that? But our true Mother Jesus, he alone bears us for joy and for endless life, blessed may he be. So he carries us within him in love and travail, until the full time when he wanted to suffer the sharpest thorns and cruel pains that ever were or will be, and at last he died. . . .

The mother can lay her child tenderly to her breast, but our tender Mother Jesus can lead us easily into his blessed breast through his sweet open side, and show us there a part of the godhead and of the joys of heaven, with inner certainty of endless bliss. . . .

This fair, lovely word *mother* is so sweet and so kind in itself that it cannot truly be said of anyone or to anyone except of him and to him who is the true Mother of life and of all things.

Julian of Norwich

Every Sort of Thing
Will Be All Right

On one occasion the good Lord said, "Everything is going to be all right." On another, "You will see for yourself that every sort of thing will be all right." In these two sayings the soul discerns various meanings.

One is that he wants us to know that not only does he care for great and noble things, but equally for little and small, lowly and simple things as well. This is his meaning: "Everything will be all right." We are to know that the least thing will not be forgotten.

Another is this: We see deeds done that are so evil, and injuries inflicted that are so great, that it seems to us quite impossible that any good can come of them. As we consider these, sorrowfully and mournfully, we cannot relax in the blessed contemplation of God as we ought. This is caused by the fact that our reason is now so blind, base, and ignorant that we are unable to know that supreme and marvelous wisdom, might, and goodness that belong to the blessed Trinity. This is the meaning of his words "You will see for yourself that every sort of thing will be all right." It is as if he were saying, "Be careful now to believe and trust, and in the end your will see it all in its fullness and joy."

Julian of Norwich

The Soul as a Living Mirror

At the beginning of the world, when God resolved to create the first being, he said in the Trinity of Persons: "Let us make man to our image and to our likeness" (Genesis 1:26). God is a spirit, so his word is his knowledge and his action is his will. He is able to do all that he wills, and all his acts are full of grace and good order. He has created each person's soul as a living mirror, on which he has impressed the image of his nature. In this way he lives imaged forth in us and we in him, for our created life is one, without intermediary, with this image and life that we have eternally in God. That life that we have in God is one in God, without intermediary, for it lives in the Father with the unbegotten Son and is begotten with the Son from the Father, flowing forth from them both with the Holy Spirit. We thus live eternally in God and he in us, for our created being lives in our eternal image, which we have in the Son of God. This eternal image is one with God's wisdom and lives in our created being.

For this reason the eternal birth is always renewed, and the flowing forth of the Holy Spirit into the emptiness of our soul is always occurring without interruption, for God has known, loved, called, and chosen us from all eternity. If we resolve to know, love, and choose him in return, then we are holy, blessed, and chosen from all eternity. Our heavenly Father will then reveal his divine resplendence in the topmost part of our soul, for we are his kingdom, in which he lives and reigns. Just as the sun in the heavens pervades and enlightens all the world with its rays and makes it fruitful, so too does God's resplendence as it reigns in the topmost part of our mind, for upon all our powers it sheds its bright, brilliant rays, namely its divine gifts: knowledge, wisdom, clear understanding, and a rational, discerning insight into all the virtues. It is in this way that the kingdom of God in our soul is adorned.

For its part, that infinite love that is God himself reigns in the purity of our spirit like the glow of burning coals. It sends forth brilliant, burning sparks which, in the fire of love, touch and enflame the heart and senses, the will and desires, and all the powers of the soul to a stormy transport of restless, formless love. These are the weapons with which we must do battle against the awesome, immense love of God, which strives to burn up and devour all loving spirits in their very being. Nevertheless God's love arms us with its own gifts, enlightening our reason and commanding, advising, and teaching us to defend ourselves in the struggle and to maintain our own rights in love against it as long as we can. For this purpose it gives us fortitude, knowledge, and wisdom, and it draws all our sensible powers together into an experience of interior fervor. It makes our heart love, desire, and savor, gives our soul the power to fix its gaze in contemplation, bestows upon us the gift of devotion, and makes us ascend on its fiery flames. It also gives knowledge and the taste of eternal wisdom to our understanding, touches our amorous power, and makes our spirit burn and melt away in veneration before its face.

Here our reason and every activity characterized by the making of distinctions must give way, for our powers now become simply one in love, grow silent, and incline toward the Father's face, since this revelation of the Father raises the soul above reason to a state of imageless bareness. There the soul is simple, spotless, and pure, empty of everything. In this pure emptiness the Father reveals his divine resplendence, which neither reason nor senses, neither rational observation nor distinctions can attain. Rather, all these things must remain below, for this infinite resplendence so blinds the eyes of reason that they have to give way before this incomprehensible light. However, that simple eye that dwells above reason in the ground of our understanding is always open, contemplating with unhindered vision and gazing at the light with the light itself — eye to eye, mirror to mirror, image to image.

With these three — eye, mirror, and image — we are like God and united with him, for this vision in our simple eye is a living mirror which God created to his image and on which he impressed his image. His image is his divine resplendence, with which he fills the mirror of our soul to overflowing, so that no other light or image can enter there. But this resplendence is not an intermediary between God and ourselves, for it is both the very thing that we see and also the light with which we see, though it is distinct from our eye that does the seeing. Even though God's image is in the mirror of our soul and is united with it without intermediary, still the image is not the mirror, for God does not become a creature. The union of the image in the mirror is, however, so great and so noble that the soul is called the image of God.

John Ruusbroec

Deified Souls

Because they have abandoned themselves to God in doing, in leaving undone, and in suffering, they have steadfast peace and inward joy, consolation and savor, of which the world cannot partake; neither any dissembler nor the man who seeks and means himself more than the glory of God. Moreover, those same inward and enlightened men have before them in their inward seeing, whenever they will, the Love of God as something drawing or urging them into the Unity; for they see and feel that the Father with the Son through the Holy Ghost embrace each other and all the chosen, and draw themselves back with eternal love into the unity of their Nature. Thus the Unity is ever drawing to itself and inviting to itself everything that has been born of it, either by nature or by grace. And therefore, too, such enlightened men are, with a free spirit, lifted up above reason into a bare and imageless vision, wherein lives the eternal indrawing summons of the Divine Unity; and, with an imageless and bare understanding, they pass through all works, and all exercises, and all things, until they reach the summit of their spirits.

There, their bare understanding is drenched through by the Eternal Brightness, even as the air is drenched through by the sunshine. And the bare, uplifted will is transformed and drenched through by abysmal love, even as iron is by fire. And the bare, uplifted memory feels itself enwrapped and established in an abysmal Absence of Image. And thereby the created image is united above reason in a threefold way with its Eternal Image, which is the origin of its being and its life.

Yet the creature does not become God, for the union takes place in God through grace and our homeward-turning love: and therefore the creature in its inward contemplation feels a distinction and an otherness between itself and God. And though the union is without means, yet the manifold works that God works in heaven and on earth are nevertheless hidden from the spirit. For though God gives himself as he is, with clear discernment, he gives himself in the essence of the soul, where the powers of the soul are simplified above reason, and where, in simplicity, they suffer the transformation of God. There all is full and overflowing, for the spirit feels itself to be one truth and one richness and one unity with God. Yet even here there is an essential tending forward, and therein is an essential distinction between the being of the soul and the Being of God; and this is the highest and finest distinction that we are able to feel.

John Ruusbroec

Both Work and Rest,
Action and Fruition

The Divine Persons who form one sole God are in the fecundity of their nature ever active; and in the simplicity of their essence they form the Godhead and eternal blessedness. Thus God according to the Persons is Eternal Work: but according to the essence and its perpetual stillness, he is Eternal Rest. Now love and fruition live between this activity and this rest. . . .

Our activity consists in loving God and our fruition in enduring God and being penetrated by his love. There is a distinction between love and fruition, as there is between God and his Grace. When we unite ourselves to God by love, then we are spirit; but when we are caught up and transformed by his Spirit, then we are led into fruition. And the spirit of God himself breathes us out from himself that we may love and may do good works; and again he draws us into himself, that we may rest in fruition. And this is Eternal Life; even as our mortal life subsists in the indrawing and outgoing of our breath. . . .

Understand, God comes to us incessantly, both with

means and without means; and he demands of us both action and fruition, in such a way that the action never hinders the fruition, nor the fruition the action, but they strengthen one another. And this is why the interior man lives his life according to these two ways; that is to say, in rest and in work. And in each of them he is wholly and undividedly; for he dwells wholly in God in virtue of his restful fruition and wholly in himself in virtue of his active love. And God, in his communications, perpetually calls and urges him to renew both this rest and this work. And because the soul is just, it desires to pay at every instant that which God demands of it; and this is why each time it is irradiated of him, the soul turns inward in a manner that is both active and fruitive, and thus it is renewed in all virtues and ever more profoundly immersed in fruitive rest. . . .

The soul is active in all loving work, for it sees its rest. It is a pilgrim, for it sees its country. For love's sake it strives for victory, for it sees its crown. Consolation, peace, joy, beauty, and riches, all that can give delight, all this is shown to the mind illuminated in God, in spiritual similitudes and without measure. And through this vision and touch of God, love continues active. For such a just man has built up in his soul, in rest and in work, a veritable life which shall endure forever. . . . Thus this man is just, and he goes toward God by inward love, in eternal work, and he goes in God by his fruitive inclination in eternal rest. And he dwells in God; and yet he goes out toward all creatures, in a spirit of love toward all things, in virtue and in works of righteousness. And this is the supreme summit of the inner life.

John Ruusbroec

Me in You and You in Me

O eternal Trinity, fire and abyss of charity, dissolve this very day the cloud of my body! I am driven to desire, in the knowledge of yourself that you have given me in your truth, to leave behind the weight of this body of mine and give my life for the glory and praise of your name. For by the light of understanding within your light I have tasted and seen your depth, eternal Trinity, and the beauty of your creation. Then, when I consider myself in you, I saw that I am in your image. You have gifted me with power from yourself, eternal Father, and my understanding with your wisdom — such wisdom as is proper to your only-begotten Son; and the Holy Spirit, who proceeds from you and from your Son, has given me a will, and so I am able to love.

You, eternal Trinity, are the craftsman; and I your handiwork have come to know that you are in love with the beauty of what you have made, since you made of me a new creation in the blood of your Son.

O abyss! O eternal Godhead! O deep sea! What more could you have given me than the gift of your very self?

You are a fire always burning but never consuming; you are a fire consuming in your heat all the soul's selfish love; you are a fire lifting all chill and giving light. In your light you have made me know your truth: You are that light beyond all light who gives the mind's eye supernatural light in such fullness and perfection that you bring clarity even to the light of faith. In that faith I see that my soul has life, and in that light receives you who are Light. . . .

Truly this light is a sea, for it nourishes the soul in you, peaceful sea, eternal Trinity. Its water is not sluggish; so the soul is not afraid because she knows the truth. It distills, revealing hidden things, so that here, where the most abundant light of your faith abounds, the soul has, as it were, a guarantee of what she believes. This water is a mirror in which you, eternal Trinity, grant me knowledge; for when I look into this mirror, holding it in the hand of love, it shows me myself, as your creation, in you, and you in me through the union you have brought about of the Godhead with our humanity.

Saint Catherine of Siena

The Spiritual Marriage

The Lord appears in this center of the soul, not in an imaginative vision but in an intellectual one, although more delicate than those mentioned, as he appeared to the apostles without entering through the door when he said to them pax vobis (peace be unto you). What God communicates here to the soul in an instant is a secret so great and a favor so sublime — and the delight the soul experiences so extreme — that I don't know what to compare it to. I can say only that the Lord wishes to reveal for that moment, in a more sublime manner than through any spiritual vision or taste, the glory of heaven. One can say no more — insofar as can be understood — than that the soul, I mean the spirit, is made one with God. For since his Majesty is also spirit, he has wished to show his love for us by giving some persons understanding of the point to which this love reaches so that we might praise his grandeur. For he has desired to be joined with the creature that, just as those who are married cannot be separated, he doesn't want to be separated from the soul.

The spiritual betrothal is different, for the two often

separate. And the union is also different because, even though it is the joining of two things into one, in the end the two can be separated and each remains by itself. We observe this ordinarily, for the favor of union with the Lord passes quickly, and afterward the soul remains without that company; I mean, without awareness of it. In this other favor from the Lord, no. The soul always remains with its God in that center. Let us say that the union is like the joining of two wax candles to such an extent that the flame coming from them is but one, or that the wick, the flame, and the wax are all one. But afterward one candle can be easily separated from the other and there are two candles; the same hold for the wick. In the spiritual marriage the union is like what we have when rain falls from the sky into a river or fount; all is water, for the rain that fell from heaven cannot be divided or separated from the water of the river. Or it is like what we have when a little stream enters the sea, there is no means of separating the two. Or, like the bright light entering a room through two different windows; although the streams of light are separate when entering the room, they become one.

Saint Teresa of Ávila

Mary and Martha Must Combine

It will be good, Sisters, to tell you the reason the Lord grants so many favors in this world. Although, if you have paid attention, you will have understood this in learning of their effects. I want to tell you again here lest someone think that the reason is solely for the sake of giving delight to these souls; that thought would be a serious error. His Majesty couldn't grant us a greater favor than to give us a life that would be an imitation of the life his beloved Son lived. Thus I hold for certain that these favors are meant to fortify our weakness, that we may be able to imitate him in his great sufferings.

We have always seen that those who were closest to Christ our Lord were those with the greatest trials. Let us look at what his glorious Mother suffered and the glorious apostles. How do you think Saint Paul could have suffered such very great trials? Through him we can see the effects visions and contemplation produce when from our Lord and not from the imagination or the devil's deceit. Did Saint Paul by chance hide himself in the enjoyment of these delights and not engage in anything else? You already see that he didn't have a day of rest, from what we can understand, and neither did he have any rest at night since it was that he earned his livelihood.

O my Sisters! How forgetful this soul, in which the Lord dwells in so particular a way, should be of its own rest, how little it should care for its honor, and how far it should be from wanting esteem in anything! For if it is with him very much, as it is right, it should think little about itself. All its concern is taken up with how to please him more and how or where it will show him the love it bears him. This is the reason for prayer, my daughters, the purpose of this spiritual marriage: the birth always of good works, good works.

I repeat, it is necessary that your foundation consist of more than prayer and contemplation. If you do not strive for the virtues and practice them, you will always be dwarfs. So be occupied in prayer not for the sake of enjoyment but so as to have the strength to serve. Mary and Martha must combine.

Saint Teresa of Ávila

DARK NIGHT

On a dark secret night,
starving for love and deep in flame,
O happy lucky flight!
unseen I slipped away,
my house at last was calm and safe.

Blackly free from light,
disguised and down a secret way,
O happy lucky flight!
in darkness I escaped,
my house at last was calm and safe.

On that happy night — in
secret; no one saw me through the dark —
and I saw nothing then,
no other light to mark
the way but fire pounding my heart.

That flaming guided me
more firmly than the noonday sun,
and waiting there was he
I knew so well — who shone
where nobody appeared to come.

O night, my guide!
O night more friendly than the dawn!
O tender night that tied
lover and the loved one,
loved one in the lover fused as one!

On my flowering breasts
which I had saved for him alone,
he slept and I caressed
and fondled him with love,
and cedars fanned the air above.

Wind from the castle wall
while my fingers played in his hair:
its hand serenely fell
wounding my neck, and there
my senses vanished in the air.

I lay. Forgot my being,
and on my love I leaned my face.
All ceased. I left my being,
leaving my cares to fade
among the lilies far away.

Saint John of the Cross

The Purification of the Fire

Before this Divine fire of love is introduced into the substance of the soul, and is united with it, by means of a purity and purgation that is perfect and complete, this flame is wounding the soul, and destroying and consuming in it the imperfections of its evil habits; and this is the operation of the Holy Spirit, wherein he prepares it for Divine union and the transformation of its substance in God through love. For the same fire of love that afterwards is united with the soul and glorifies it is that which aforetime assailed it in order to purge it; even as the fire that penetrates the log of wood is the same that first of all attacked and wounded it with its flame, cleansing and stripping it of its accidents of ugliness, until, by means of its heat, it had prepared it to such a degree that it could enter it and transform it into itself. In this operation the soul endures great suffering and experiences grievous afflictions in its spirit, which at times overflow into the senses, at which times this flame is very oppressive. For in this preparatory state of purgation the flame is not bright to it, but dark. Neither is it sweet to it, but grievous; for, although at times it kindles within it the heat of love, this is accompanied by torment and affliction. And it is not delectable to it, but arid; it brings it neither refreshment nor peace, but consumes and accuses it; neither is it glorious to it, but rather it makes it miserable and bitter, by means of the spiritual light of self-knowledge that it sheds upon it, for God sends fire, as Jeremiah says, into its bones, and tries it by fire, as David says likewise.

And thus at this time the soul also suffers great darkness in the understanding, many aridities and afflictions in the will, and grievous knowledge of its miseries in the memory, for the eye of its spiritual self-knowledge is very bright. And in its substance the soul suffers profoundly from its poverty and abandonment.

Now, since this is the remedy and medicine that God gives to the soul for its many infirmities, that he may bring it health, the soul must needs suffer in the purgation and remedy, according to the nature of its sickness. For here its heart is laid upon the coals, so that every kind of evil spirit is driven away from it; and here its infirmities are continually brought to light and are laid bare before its eyes that it may feel them, and then they are cured. And that which aforetime was hidden and set deep within the soul is now seen and felt by it, in the light and heat of the fire, whereas aforetime it saw nothing. Even so, in the water and smoke that the fire drives out of wood are seen the humidity and the frigidity that it had aforetime, though this was realized by none. But now, being brought near to this flame, the soul clearly sees and feels its miseries, for — oh, wonderful thing! — there arise within it contraries against contraries against contraries, some of which, as the philosophers say, bring the others to light; and they make war in the soul, striving to expel each other in order that they may reign within it.

God, who is all perfection, wars against all the imperfect habits of the soul, and, purifying the soul with the heat of his flame, he uproots its habits from it, and prepares it, so that at last he may enter it and be united with it by his sweet, peaceful, and glorious love, as is the fire when it has entered the wood.

Saint John of the Cross

The Elixir

Teach me, my God and King,
In all things thee to see,
And what I do in any thing
To do it as for thee.

Not rudely, as a beast,
To runne into an action;
But still to make thee prepossest,
And give it his perfection.

A man that looks on glasse,
On it may stay his eye;
Or if he pleaseth, through it passe,
And then the heav'n espie.

All may of thee partake:
Nothing can be so mean
Which with his tincture, "for Thy sake,"
Will not grow bright and clean.

A servant with this clause
Makes drudgerie divine;
Who sweeps a room as for thy laws
Makes that and th' action fine.

This is the famous stone
That turneth all to gold;
For that which God doth touch and own
Cannot for lesse be told.

George Herbert

THE HOUSE OF GOD

Your enjoyment of the world is never right, till every morning you awake in Heaven; see yourself in your Father's Palace; and look upon the skies, the earth, and the air as Celestial Joys: having such a reverend esteem of all, as if you were among the Angels. The bride of a monarch, in her husband's chamber, hath no such causes of delight as you.

You never enjoy the world aright, till the Sea itself floweth in your veins, till you are clothed with the heavens, and crowned with the stars: and perceive yourself to be the sole heir of the whole world, and more than so, because men are in it who are every one sole heirs as well as you. Till you can sing and rejoice and delight in God, as misers do in gold, and Kings in scepters, you never enjoy the world.

Till your spirit filleth the whole world, and the stars are your jewels; till you are as familiar with the ways of God in all Ages as with your walk and table; till you are intimately acquainted with that shady nothing out of which the world was made; till you love men so as to desire their happiness, with a thirst equal to the zeal of your own; till you delight in God for being good to all: you never enjoy the world. Till you more feel it than your private estate, and are more present in the hemisphere, considering the glories and the beauties there, than in your own house; till you remember how lately you were made, and how wonderful it was when you came into it; and more rejoice in the palace of your glory, than if it had been made but today morning.

Yet further, you never enjoy the world aright, till you so love the beauty of enjoying it, that you are covetous and earnest to persuade others to enjoy it. . . . The world is a mirror of infinite beauty, yet no man sees it. It is a Temple of Majesty, yet no man regards it. It is a region of Light and Peace, did not men disquiet it. It is the Paradise of God. It is more to man since he is fallen than it was before. It is the place of Angels and the Gate of Heaven. When Jacob waked out of his dream, he said "God is here, and I wist it not. How dreadful is this place! This is none other than the House of God and the Gate of Heaven."

Thomas Traherne

THE KNOT

Bright Queen of Heaven! Gods Virgin Spouse
    The glad worlds blessed maid!
Whose beauty tyed life to thy house,
    And brought us saving ayd.

Thou art the true Loves-knot; by thee
    God is made our Allie,
And mans inferior Essence he
    With his did dignifie.

For Coalescent by that Band
    We are his body grown,
Nourished with favors from his hand
    Whom for our head we own.

And such a Knot, what arm dares loose,
    What life, what death can sever?
Which us in him, and him in us
    United keeps for ever.

Henry Vaughan

I Must Be the Virgin and Give Birth to God

What does it matter to me if Gabriel salute the Virgin
If he does not also bring me the same marvellous news?

God is the Light of Light, my saviour is the sun,
The Virgin is the moon, and I am their secret joy.

Know that God becomes a child, lies in the virgin's womb
So I can grow like him, and gather to me Godhead.

When God lay hidden in a young virgin's womb
Then a miracle occurred; the point contained the circle.

Virginity is noble, but a mother you must also be
Or be a field stripped bare of all fertility.

The Virgin is a crystal, her son divine Light:
She is utterly pierced by him, yet stays untouched.

I must be the Virgin and give birth to God
Should I ever be graced divine beatitude.

Angelus Silesius

Dearest and Holiest and Most Beloved Mother

If you still see in me something that does not belong
   to you
I beg you to take it out this moment
And to make yourself the absolute mistress of my being
And all its powers
And to destroy, uproot, annihilate, transmute, and
   transform
Everything in me that displeases God
And to plant in its place and make grow and make
   flourish
Everything that pleases you.
May the light of your faith dissipate the darkness of my
   spirit.
May your profound humility take the place of my
   arrogance.
May your sublime contemplativeness
Halt the distractions of my vagabond imagination.
May your continual vision of God fill my memory with
   divine presence.

May the blaze of your heart's charity
Dilate and inflame the lethargy and frigidity of mine.
May your virtues take the place of my imperfections.
May your merits be my ornament and advocate before
  God.
Dearest and holiest and most beloved Mother,
See to it that I have no other spirit but yours
To know Jesus Christ and his divine commands,
That I have no other soul but yours with which to praise
  and glorify God,
That I have no other heart but yours
To love God with a pure and ardent love like yours.

Saint Louis-Marie Grignion de Montfort

MARY AND THE SECOND COMING
OF CHRIST

It is through the Very Holy Virgin that Jesus Christ came into the world to begin with, and it is also through her that he will reign in the world. . . .

I say with the saints; the divine Mary is the terrestrial paradise of the New Adam, where he was incarnate by the operation of the Holy Spirit to work incomprehensible miracles, she is the great, divine world of God where there are ineffable beauties and treasures. She is the magnificence of the Most High where he has hidden, as if in his own breast, his only Son. . . . O! How many great and hidden things all-powerful God has made in this wonderful woman. . . .

Until now, the divine Mary has been unknown, and this is one of the reasons why Jesus Christ is hardly known as he should be. If then — as is certain — the knowledge and reign of Jesus Christ arrive in the world, it will be a necessary consequence of the knowledge and reign of the Very Holy Virgin, who birthed him into this world the first time and will make him burst out everywhere the second.

Jesus Christ is for every person who possesses him the fruit and the work of Mary.... When Mary has put down her roots in a soul she engenders there miracles of grace that she alone can work, for she alone is the fecund Virgin who has never had and never will have any equal in purity or fecundity.... Mary has produced, with the Holy Spirit, the greatest thing that has ever been — or will ever be — the God-man, and she will produce the greatest things that shall be in these last times. The formation and education of the heroic saints that will come at the end of the world are reserved for her; for only this singular and miraculous Virgin can produce, in union with the Holy Spirit, singular and extraordinary things....

Mary must break out more than ever in these last times in pity, force, and grace. Her power over the demons will flash out everywhere.... It is a kind of miracle when a person remains firm in the middle of the fierce torrent of these times, and strays uninfected in the plague-ridden air of our corrupt era.... It is the Virgin, in whom the Serpent has never had any part, that works this miracle for those beings who love her well.

Anyone who knows Mary as Mother and submits to her and obeys her in all things will soon grow very rich; every day, he or she will amass treasures, by the secret power of her philosopher's stone. "He who glorifies his Mother is like one who amasses treasure.". . . It is in the bosom of Mary that the young become old in light and holiness and experience and wisdom. . . .

Mary is the dawn that precedes and reveals the Sun of Justice. . . . The difference between the first and second coming of Jesus will be that the first was secret and hidden, the second will be glorious and dazzling; both will be perfect, because both will come through Mary. This is a great and holy mystery that no one can understand; "let all tongues here fall silent."

Saint Louis-Marie Grignion de Montfort

The Treasure

What is the secret of finding the Treasure? There isn't one. The Treasure is everywhere. It is offered to us at every moment and wherever we find ourselves. All creatures, friends or enemies, pour it out abundantly, and it courses through every fiber of our body and soul until it reaches the very core of our being. If we open our mouths they will be filled. God's activity runs through the entire universe. It wells up around and penetrates every created being. Wherever they are, it is there also. It runs ahead of them, it stays with them, and it follows after them. All they have to do is to allow its waves to sweep them forward, fulfill the simple duties of their religion and status in life, accept cheerfully all the difficulties they meet, and surrender to the will of God in all they have to do.... This is authentic spirituality, and it is valid for all times and for everyone. We could not choose to become good in a better, more miraculous, and yet easier way than by the simple use of the means offered us by God; the whole-hearted acceptance of everything that comes to us at every moment of our lives.

Jean Pierre de Caussade

His Work Is Perfect

Our task is to offer ourselves up to God like a clean, smooth canvas and not bother ourselves about what God may choose to paint on it, but, at every moment, feel only the stroke of his brush. It is the same with a piece of stone. Each blow from the chisel of the sculptor makes it feel — if it could feel — if it were being destroyed. As blow after blow rains down on it, the stone knows nothing about how the sculptor is shaping it. All it feels is a chisel hacking away at it, savaging it and mutilating it.

Let us take, for example, a piece of stone that is destined to be carved into a crucifix or a statue. We might ask it: "What do you think is happening to you?" And it might well answer: "Why are you asking me? All I know is that I must stay immobile in the hands of the sculptor. I have no notion of what he is doing, nor do I know what he will make of me. What I do know, however, is that his work is the finest imaginable. It is perfect. I welcome each blow of his chisel as the best thing that could happen to me, although, if I am to tell the complete truth, I feel that every one of these blows is ruining me, destroying me, and disfiguring me."

Jean Pierre de Caussade

To the Christians

I know of no other Christianity and of no other Gospel than the liberty both of body and mind to exercise the Divine Arts of Imagination. Imagination the real and eternal World of which this Vegetable Universe is but a faint shadow and in which we shall live in our Eternal or Imaginative Bodies, when these Vegetable Mortal Bodies are no more. The Apostles knew of no other Gospel. What were all their spiritual gifts? What is the Divine Spirit? is the Holy Ghost any other than an Intellectual Fountain: What is the Harvest of the Gospel and its Labors? What is that Talent which it is a curse to hide? What are the Treasures of Heaven that we are to lay up for ourselves, are they any other than Mental Studies and Performances? What are all the Gifts of the Gospel, are they not all Mental Gifts? Is God a Spirit who must be worshipped in Spirit and in Truth, and are not the Gifts of the Spirit Everything to Man? . . . Answer this to yourselves, and expel from among you those who pretend to despise the labors of Art and Science which alone are the labors of the Gospel: Is not this plain and manifest to the thought?

Can you think at all and not pronounce heartily! That to Labor in Knowledge, is to Build up Jerusalem: and to Despise Knowledge, is to Despise Jerusalem and her Builders. And remember: He who despises and mocks a Mental Gift in another; calling it pride and selfishness and sin; mocks Jesus the giver of every Mental Gift, which always appear to the ignorance-loving Hypocrite, as Sins; but that which is a Sin in the sight of cruel Man, is not so in the sight of our kind God. Let every Christian, as much as in him lies, engage himself openly and publicly before all the World in some Mental pursuit for the Building up of Jerusalem.

> I stood among my valleys of the south
> And saw a flame of fire, even as a Wheel
> Of fire surrounding all the heavens: it went
> From west to east against the current of
> Creation and devoured all things in its loud
> Fury and thundering course round heaven and earth.
> By it the Sun was rolld into an orb;
> By it the Moon faded into a globe,
> Traveling thro the night: for from its dire
> And restless fury, Man himself shrunk up
> Into a little root a fathom long.
> And I asked a Watcher and a Holy One
> Its Name? he answered. It is the Wheel of Religion

I wept and said. Is this the law of Jesus,
This terrible devouring sword turning every way
He answered; Jesus died because he strove
Against the current of this Wheel: its Name
Is Caiaphas, the dark Preacher of Death
Of sin, of sorrow, and of punishment;
Opposing Nature! It is Natural Religion
But Jesus is the bright Preacher of Life
Creating Nature from this fiery Law,
By self-denial and forgiveness of Sin.
Go therefore, cast out devils in Christ's name
Heal thou the sick of spiritual disease
Pity the evil, for thou art not sent
To smite with terror and with punishments
Those that are sick, like to the Pharisees
Crucifying and encompassing sea and land
For proselytes to tyranny and wrath.
But to the Publicans and Harlots go!
Teach them True Happiness, but let no curse
Go forth out of thy mouth to blight their peace
For Hell is opened to Heaven; thine eyes beheld
The dungeons burst and the Prisoners set free.

William Blake

The Divine Image

To Mercy, Pity, Peace, and Love
All pray in their distress;
And to these virtues of delight
Return their thankfulness.

For Mercy, Pity, Peace, and Love
Is God, our Father dear,
And Mercy, Pity, Peace, and Love
Is man, his child and care.

For Mercy has a human heart,
Pity a human face,
And Love, the human form divine,
And Peace, the human dress.

Then every man, of every clime,
That prays in his distress,
Prays to the human form divine,
Love, Mercy, Pity, Peace.

And all must love the human form,
In heathen, Turk, or Jew;
Where Mercy, Love, and Pity dwell
There God is dwelling too.

William Blake

Auguries of Innocence

To see a World in a grain of sand,
And a Heaven in a wild flower,
Hold Infinity in the palm of your hand,
And Eternity in an hour . . .

The bat that flits at close of eve
Has left the brain that won't believe.
The owl that calls upon the night
Speaks the unbeliever's fright . . .

Joy and woe are woven fine,
A clothing for the soul divine;
Under every grief and pine
Runs a joy with silken twine . . .

Every tear from every eye
Becomes a babe in Eternity . . .

The bleat, the bark, bellow, and roar
Are waves that beat on Heaven's shore . . .

He who doubts from what he sees
Will ne'er believe, do what you please.
If the Sun and Moon should doubt,
They'd immediately go out . . .

God appears, and God is Light,
To those poor souls who dwell in Night;
But does a Human Form display
To those who dwell in realms of Day.

William Blake

THE HOLY CONVERSATION BETWEEN SAINT SERAPHIM OF SAROV AND MOTOVILOV

"How," I asked Father Seraphim, "can I know that I am in the grace of the Holy Spirit? I do not understand how I can be certain that I am in the Spirit of God. How can I discern for myself his true manifestation in me?"

Father Seraphim replied: "I have already told you, Your Godliness, that it is very simple and I have related in detail how people come to be in the Spirit of God and how we can recognize his presence in us. So what do you want, my son?" "I want to understand it well," I said. Then Father Seraphim took me very firmly by the shoulders and said: "We are both in the Spirit of God now, my son. Why don't you look at me?" I replied: "I cannot look, Batiushka, because your eyes are flashing like lightning. Your face has become brighter than the sun, and my eyes ache with pain."

Father Seraphim said: "Don't be alarmed, Your Godliness! Now you yourself have become as bright as I am. You are now in the fullness of the Spirit of God yourself;

otherwise you would not be able to see me as I am." Then bending his head toward me, he whispered softly in my ear: "Thank the Lord God for his unutterable mercy to us! You saw that I did not even cross myself; and only in my heart I prayed mentally to the Lord and said within myself: 'Lord, grant him to see clearly with his bodily eyes that descent of thy Spirit which thou grantest to thy servants when thou art pleased to appear in the light of thy magnificent glory.' And you see my son, the Lord instantly fulfilled the humble prayer of poor Seraphim. How then shall we not thank him for this unspeakable gift to us both? Even to the greatest hermits, my son, the Lord God does not always show his mercy in this way. This grace of God, like a loving mother, has been pleased to comfort your contrite heart at the intercession of the Mother of God herself. But why, my son, do you not look me in the eyes? Just look, and don't be afraid! The Lord is with us!"

After these words I glanced at his face and there came over me an even greater reverent awe. Imagine in the center of the sun, in the dazzling light of its midday rays, the face of a man talking to you. You see the movement of his lips and the changing expression of his eyes, you hear his voice, you feel someone holding your shoulders; yet you do not see his hands, you do not even see yourself or his figure, but only a blinding light spreading far around for several yards and illumining with its brilliance both the snow-blanket that covered the forest glade and the snowflakes which besprinkled me and the great elder. You can imagine the state I was in!

"How do you feel now?" Father Seraphim asked me.

"Extraordinarily well," I said.

"But in what way? How exactly do you feel well?"

I answered: "I feel such calmness and peace in my soul that no words can express it."

"This, Your Godliness," said Father Seraphim, "is that peace of which the Lord said to his disciples; 'My peace I give unto you: not as the world giveth, give I unto you' (John 14:27). What else do you feel?" Father Seraphim asked me. "An extraordinary sweetness," I replied.

And he continued: "This is that sweetness of which it is said in Holy Scripture: 'They shall be drunken with the fatness of thy house, and of the torrent of thy delight shalt thou make them to drink' (Psalm 36:8). And now this sweetness is flooding our hearts. . . . What else do you feel?" "An extraordinary joy in all my heart."

And Father Seraphim continued: "When the Spirit of God comes down to man and overshadows him with the fullness of his inspiration, then the human soul overflows with unspeakable joy, for the Spirit of God fills with joy whatever he touches. You my son, have wept enough in your life on earth; yet see with what joy the Lord consoles you even in this life! What else do you feel, Your Godliness?"

I answered: "An extraordinary warmth."

"How can you feel warmth, my son? Look, we are sitting in the forest. It is winter out-of-doors, and snow is under-foot. There is more than an inch of snow on us, and the snowflakes are still falling. What warmth can there be?"

I answered: "Such as there is in a bathhouse when the water is poured on the stone and the steam rises in clouds." "And the smell," he asked me, "is it like the smell of a bathhouse?"

"No," I replied. "There is nothing on earth like this fragrance. When in my dear mother's lifetime I was fond of dancing and used to go to balls and parties, my mother would sprinkle me with the scent that she bought at the best shops in Kazan. But those scents did not exhale such fragrance."

And Father Seraphim, smiling pleasantly, said: "I know it myself just as well as you do, my son, but I am asking you on purpose to see whether you feel it in the same way. It is absolutely true, Your Godliness! The sweetest earthly fragrance cannot be compared with the fragrance that we now feel, for we are now enveloped in the fragrance of the Holy Spirit of God. . . .

"Our present state is that of which the Apostle says, The Kingdom of God is not meat and drink; but righteousness, and peace in the Holy Spirit' (Romans 14:17). Our faith consists not in the plausible words of earthly wisdom but in the demonstration of the Spirit and power (see I Corinthians 2:4). That is just the state we are in now. Of this state the Lord said, There are some of them that stand here, which shall not taste of death, till they have seen the Kingdom of God come with power' (Mark 9:1). See, my son, what unspeakable joy the Lord God has now granted us!"

"I don't know Batiushka," I said, "whether the Lord will grant me to remember this mercy of God always as vividly and clearly as I feel it now. 'I think,' Father Seraphim answered me, 'that the Lord will help you to retain it in your memory forever, or his goodness would never have instantly bowed in this way to my humble prayer and so quickly anticipated the request of poor Seraphim; all the more so, because it is not given to you alone to understand it, but through you it is for the whole world, in order that you yourself may be confirmed in God's work and may be useful to others. The fact that I am a monk and you are a layman is utterly beside the point. What God requires is true faith in himself and his only-begotten Son. In return for that the grace of the Holy Spirit is granted abundantly from on high. The Lord seeks a heart filled to overflowing with love for God and our neighbor; this is the throne on which he loves to sit and on which he appears in the fullness of his heavenly glory. Son, give me thine heart (Proverbs 23:26; see Matthew 6:33), for in the human heart the Kingdom of God can be contained.'"

N. A. Motovilov

The Magic of the Name of Jesus

When I prayed with my heart, everything around me seemed delightful and marvelous. The trees, the grass, the birds, the earth, the air, the light seemed to be telling me that they existed for man's sake, that they witnessed to the love of God for man, that everything proved the love of God for man, that all things prayed to God and sang his praise.

Sometimes my understanding, which had been so stupid before, was given so much light that I could easily grasp and dwell upon matters of which up to now I had not been able even to think at all. Sometimes that sense of a warm gladness in my heart spread throughout my whole being and I was deeply moved as the fact of the presence of God everywhere was brought home to me. Sometimes by calling upon the name of Jesus I was overwhelmed with bliss, and now I knew the meaning of the words "The kingdom of God is within you."

The Prayer of my heart gave me such consolation that I felt there was no happier person on earth than I, and I doubted if there could be greater and fuller happiness in the kingdom of Heaven. Not only did I feel this in my own soul, but the whole outside world also seemed to me full of charm and delight. Everything drew me to love and thank God: people, trees, plants, animals. I saw them all as my kinsfolk, I found in all of them the magic of the Name of Jesus.

from *The Way of a Pilgrim*

TRUE CHRISTIANITY

True Christianity is the regeneration of mankind and the world in the spirit of Christ, the transformation of the kingdom of this world into the Kingdom of God, which is not of this world. This regeneration is a long and complex process. It cannot be simply a natural process or one that happens by itself, unconsciously. It is a *spiritual process*, and it is necessary that humanity participate in *it by means of a man's own faculties and mental forces....*

The Spirit of Christ blows wherever it wills. Indeed, *even its foes* may serve it. Christ has required us to love our enemies, and therefore he not only is able to love them, but certainly realizes *how to make use of them* in his work. Those unbelieving workers in the case of modern progress have nonetheless worked for the good of Christianity. They could not harm Christ by their lack of belief, *but they have hurt material Nature*, with which many of them were working. They express the false view that Nature is lifeless matter, a machine without a soul. In return, Nature, as if insulted by this twofold lie, *refuses to feed humanity.* It is this common danger that should unite both believers and unbelievers.

It is time men realized their oneness with Mother Earth and rescued her from lifelessness, so they also can save *themselves* from death. But what oneness can we have with the earth, when we have no such oneness, no such moral *relationships among ourselves*?

It is easy to blame others, to hamper them. Seek to do better yourselves to bring about a living, social, universal Christianity. If we are truly Christians *in deed* and not only in name, *it depends upon our efforts that Christ in his humanity will rise form the dead.*

Vladimir Soloviev

God's Grandeur

The world is charged with the grandeur of God.
   It will flame out, like shining from shook foil;
   It gathers to a greatness, like the ooze of oil
Crushed. Why do men then now not reck his rod?
Generations have trod, have trod, have trod;
   And all is seared with trade; bleared, smeared
      with toil;
   And wears man's smudge and shares man's smell:
      the soil
Is bare now, nor can foot feel, being shod.

And for all this, nature is never spent;
   There lives the dearest freshness deep down things;
And though the last lights of the black West went
   Oh, morning, at the brown brink eastward, springs —
Because the Holy Ghost over the bent
   World broods with warm breast and with ah! bright
      wings.

Gerard Manley Hopkins

The Blessed Virgin Compared
to the Air We Breathe

I say that we are wound
With mercy round and round
As if with air: the same
Is Mary, more by name,
She, wild web, wondrous robe,
Mantles the guilty globe.
Since God has let dispense
Her prayers his providence.
Nay, more than almoner,
The sweet alms' self is her
And men are meant to share
Her life as life does air.
    If I have understood,
She holds high motherhood
Towards all our ghostly good,
And plays in grace her part
About man's beating heart,
Laying like air's fine flood
The death-dance in his blood;

Yet no part but what will
Be Christ our Saviour still.
Of her flesh he took flesh:
He does take, fresh and fresh,
Though much the mystery how,
Not flesh but spirit now,
And wakes, O marvellous!
New Nazareths in us,
Where she shall yet conceive
Him, morning, noon, and eve;
New Bethlehems, and he born
There, evening, noon and morn.
Bethlehem or Nazareth,
Men here may draw like breath
More Christ, and baffle death;
Who, born so, comes to be
New self, and nobler me
In each one, and each one
More makes, when all is done,
Both God's and Mary's son. . . .

Gerard Manley Hopkins

The Little Way

I have always desired to become a saint, but in comparing myself with the saints I have always felt that I am as far removed from them as a grain of sand, trampled underfoot by a passer-by, is from the mountain whose peak is hidden in clouds.

Instead of feeling dismayed by such thoughts, I concluded that God would never inspire a desire that could not be realized, and that despite my littleness I might still aim at being a saint. I said to myself "It is impossible for me to become great, so I must bear with myself and my many imperfections."

But I will search out a means of attaining heaven by a little way — very short and direct, and completely new. We live, after all, in an age of inventions. There are lifts that save us the trouble of climbing stairs.

So I will try and find a lift that will raise me to God, for I am too small to climb the steep stairs of perfection.

I looked in Scripture to find some suggestion of what the lift I wanted might be. I came across these words from the Book of Proverbs: "Whoever is a little one, let that person come to me" (Proverbs 9:4). So I drew near to God, certain that I had discovered what I was looking for. I continued my search and this is what I found: "You shall be carried at the breasts and upon the knees: as one whom the mother caresses, so will I comfort you" (Isaiah 66:12–13).

I have never before been consoled with more tender or sweet words. Jesus, it is your arms then that must be the lift that will raise me to heaven. To reach heaven I do not have to become great. On the contrary I must stay little. I must become even smaller than I am.

Saint Thérèse of Lisieux

Love's Vision

At night in each other's arms,
Content, overjoyed, resting deep deep down in
    the darkness,
Lo! the heavens opened and He appeared —
Whom no mortal eye may see,
Whom no eye clouded with Care,
Whom none who seeks after this or that, whom none
    who has not escaped from self.

There — in the region of Equality, in the world of
    Freedom no longer limited,
Standing as a lofty peak in heaven above the clouds,
From below hidden, yet to all who pass into that region
    most clearly visible —
He the Eternal appeared.

                                                Edward Carpenter

THE COSMIC CHRIST

Under what form, and with what end in view, has the Creator given us, and still preserves in us, the gift of participated being? Under the form of an essential aspiration towards him — and with a view to the unhoped-for cleaving that is to make us one and the same complex thing with him. The action by which God maintains us in the field of his presence is a unitive transformation.

Let us go further still. What is the supreme and complex reality for which the divine operation moulds us? It is revealed to us by Saint Paul and Saint John. It is the quantitative repletion and the qualitative consummation of all things: It is the mysterious Pleroma, in which the substantial one and the created many fuse without confusion in a whole that, without adding anything essential to God, will nevertheless be a sort of triumph and generalization of being.

What is the active center, the living link, the organising soul of the Pleroma? Saint Paul, again, proclaims it with all his resounding voice: It is he in whom everything is reunited, and in whom all things are consummated —

through whom the whole created edifice receives its consistency — Christ dead and risen *qui replet omnia, in quo omnia constant.*

And now let us link the first and last terms of this long series of identities. We shall then see with a wave of joy that the divine omnipresence translates itself within our universe by the network of the organizing forces of the total Christ. God exerts pressure, in us and upon us — through the intermediary of all the powers of heaven, earth and hell — only in the act of forming and consummating Christ who saves and suranimates the world. And since, in the course of this operation, Christ himself does not act as a dead or passive point of convergence, but as a center of radiation of the energies that lead the universe back to God through his humanity, the layers of divine action finally come to us impregnated with his organic energies.

Pierre Teilhard de Chardin

A New Identity and
a New Mode of Action

Christ living in me is at the same time himself and myself. From the moment that I am united to him "in one spirit" there is no longer any contradiction implied by the fact that we are different persons. He remains, naturally and physically, the Son of God who was born of the blessed Virgin in Nazareth, who went about doing good, and who died on the Cross, two thousand years ago. I remain the singular person that I am. But mystically and spiritually Christ lives in me from the moment that I am united to him in his death and resurrection. . . .

This union is not merely a moral union, or an agreement of wills, nor merely a psychological union that flows from the fact that I keep him in my thoughts. Christ mystically identifies his members with himself by giving them his Holy Spirit. . . .

"I came," said Jesus, "that they may have life" (John 10:10). The life he came to bring us is his own life as Son of God. And because of his resurrection he received the power to communicate to us all his Spirit as the principle of our own life and the life of our own spirit. The un-created Image, buried and concealed by sin in the depths of our souls, rises from death when, sending forth his Spirit into our spirit, he manifests his presence within us and becomes for us the source of a new life, a new identity and a new mode of action.

Thomas Merton

Mary, the First Christian Revolutionary

The backdrop of the Magnificat is the tragic character of a world that is unjustly ordered and therefore an obstacle to God's plan for society and human beings. However, God has resolved to intervene through the Messiah and to inaugurate new relationships with all things. All Israel, and all humanity, yearn for this saving moment. Mary has understood: Now, in her womb, suddenly the principle and agent of all salvation and liberation has sprung to human life. It is as if Jesus were already exclaiming, "This is the time of fulfillment. The Reign of God is at hand! Reform your lives and believe in the gospel!" (Mark 1:15) — the cry he will one day utter as he starts enthusiastically down the highways and byways of Galilee.

Mary, too, is filled with jubilation and intones her hymn of laud and joy. Nor is her joy a kind of "whistling in the dark," fingers crossed, hoping but without a real basis for hope. No, Mary is filled with messianic exaltation. God has become the Saviour (Luke 1:47), and has looked kindly upon the lowly servant woman (Luke 1:48). And behold: Mary becomes the prototype of what God intends to do for all humanity. This is why she can sing that every generation will call her blessed (Luke 1:48).

God is the Holy, and the Utterly Other, who dwells in inaccessible light (see Luke 1:49). But God does not live at a sovereign distance, far from the excruciating cries of the children of God. The Blessed Virgin can proclaim that God's mercy extends from age to age (Luke 1:50). God has left the resplendent shadows of an inaccessible abode and now draws near the murky light of the human race. God enters the conflict, takes up the cause of the conquered and the marginalized against the mighty. God strikes down those who "make history," a history that they themselves intend to write in books filled with their self-magnification.

The mercy of God is not reserved for the end time alone. The mercy of God will not allow the wound to fester. The mercy of God takes historical forms, is made concrete in deeds that transform the interplay of forces. The proud, with the power in their hands, the wealthy, do not have the last word. They think they have, but the divine justice is already upon them, in history itself. They will be stripped of their power, the mask will be torn from their proud faces, and they will be sent away empty-handed (Luke 1:51–53). The Reign of God is anything but the consecration of this world's "law and order" — the decree of the overambitious. The Reign of God is precisely a protest against the "order" of this world. The Reign of Justice is the reign of a different justice. God promised this new world to our ancestors, and this promise is our certitude.

Leonardo Boff

THE TRADITION OF PRAISE

If I were asked to name in one word the message I have received from my religion regarding sexuality over the forty-five years of my life I would answer: regret. I believe that the Western church, following in the spirit of Saint Augustine, basically regrets the fact that we are sexual, sensual creatures. "If only sexuality would go away," the message goes, "we could get on with important issues of faith." But there is another tradition besides Saint Augustine's regarding our bodiliness and deep sexual natures — the tradition of praise. It is time that the voice of the churches joined the voices of the other creatures to praise the Creator. . . .

The Cosmic Christ might speak thus on the topic of sexuality: "Let religion and the churches abandon their efforts to be 'houses of sublimation.' Instead, reenter the cosmic mystery that sexuality is and teach your people, young and old, to do the same, remembering justice, remembering responsibility as intrinsic to the mystical experience. All lovemaking (as distinct from 'having sex') is Christ meeting Christ. Love beds are altars. People are temples encountering temples, the holy of holies receiving the holy of holies. Wings of cherubim and seraphim beat to the groans and passions of human lovers, for the cosmic powers are there eager to enhance the celebration."

Matthew Fox

Being Happy with Him Now

We all long for heaven where God is, but we have it in our power to be in heaven with him at this very moment. But being happy with him now means:

> Loving as he loves,
> Helping as he helps,
> Giving as he gives,
> Serving as he serves,
> Rescuing as he rescues,
> Being with him twenty-four hours,
> Touching him in his distressing disguise.

Mother Teresa

THE NEW CREATION

This earth and all that is in it, and the whole cosmic order to which it belongs, has to undergo a transformation; it has to become a "new heaven and a new earth." Modern physics helps us to realize that this whole material universe is a vast "field of energies" that is in a continuous process of transformation. Matter is passing into life and life into consciousness, and we are waiting for the time when our present mode of consciousness will be transformed and we shall transcend the limits of space and time, and enter "the new creation."

There is a remarkable anticipation of this view in the Letter to the Romans, where Saint Paul speaks of the whole creation "groaning in travail." For the creation, he says, "waits with eager longing for the revealing of the sons of God." The "revealing of the sons of God" is, of course, the passage of humanity into the new state of consciousness. For "we ourselves," he says "groan inwardly as we wait for the adoption of sons, the redemption of our bodies." Our adoption as sons is our passing from human to divine consciousness, which is the destiny of all humanity. And this will come through "the redemption of our bodies." The new consciousness is not a bodiless state; it is the transformation of our present body consciousness, which is limited by time and space, into a state of transformed body consciousness which is that of resurrection. In the resurrection Jesus passed from our present state of material being and consciousness, which is the destiny of all humanity.

This is the "new creation" of which Saint Paul speaks and which is revealed more explicitly in the Second Letter of Peter, where it is said, "According to his promise we await a new heaven and a new earth in which righteousness dwells." This is the ultimate goal of human history and of the created universe.

Bede Griffiths

Envoi: You Are Christ's Hands

Christ has no body now on earth but yours,
    no hands but yours,
    no feet but yours,
Yours are the eyes through which is to look out
    Christ's compassion to the world;
Yours are the feet with which he is to go about
    doing good;
Yours are the hands with which he is to bless men now.

Saint Teresa of Ávila

TEACHINGS OF
THE CHRISTIAN MYSTICS
SOURCES

SOURCES

All selections from the Gospels, the Letters of Saint Paul, and the Revelation are taken from the 1611 King James Version of the Bible.

"If You Will Not Know Yourselves," "The Sign of the Father," and "Into a Single One" are adapted from translations of the Gospel of Thomas by Anthony Duncan in *Jesus: Essential Reading* (Crucible Press, 1986).

"All Eyes, All Light, All Face, All Glory, and All Spirit" by Saint Macarius of Egypt is adapted from the translation by Evelyn Underhill in *The Mystic Way* (Atlanta, Ga.: Ariel Press, 1994).

"My Sins Are Running Out Behind Me," "To His Last Breath," "Take Care of the Sick," and "Why Not Be Utterly Changed into Fire?" are adapted from translations by Thomas Merton in *The Wisdom of the Desert* (New York: New Directions, 1965).

"Entering the Dark Cloud," "Doctrine of Infinite Growth," and "Unity in Diversity" by Gregory of Nyssa are taken from *Gregory of Nyssa's Mystical Writings,* translated and edited by Herbert Mursillo (Crestwood, N.Y.: St. Vladimir's Seminary Press, 1979).

"The Radiance of the Divine Darkness" is adapted from the translation of the *Mystical Theology* by Colm Luibheid in *Pseudo-Dionysius: The Complete Works* (Mahwah, New Jersey: Paulist Press).

"Entering into Joy" by Saint Augustine is taken from Eknath Easwaran's anthology *God Makes the Rivers to Flow* (Nilgiri Press, 1991), copyright 1991, Nilgiri Press, Tomales, CA 94971.

"She Leads Us All to Divine Knowledge" and "Healing of My Body and Salvation of My Soul" are adapted from the translation of the Akathist Hymn of Romanus the Melodist by Father Seraphim Rose in *The Orthodox Veneration of Mary, the Birthgiver of God* by Saint John Maximovitch (Platina, Calif.: St. Herman of Alaska Brotherhood, 1994).

"An Invocation to the Holy Spirit" by Saint Symeon the New Theologian is adapted from the translation by Kallistos Ware in *The Orthodox Way* (Crestwood, N.Y.: St. Vladimir's Seminary Press, 1979).

"Beyond Nature, Thought, or Conception," "Guard the Heart," and "Take the Poor Man In" by Saint Symeon the New Theologian are adapted from translations in *The Philokalia: The Complete Text*, vol. 4 (London: Faber & Faber, 1995)

"A Charitable Heart" by Saint Isaac the Syrian is taken from *The Mystical Theology of the Eastern Church* by Vladimir Lossky (Crestwood, N.Y.: St. Vladimir's Seminary Press, 1991).

"Constant Prayer" by Saint Isaac the Syrian is adapted from translations in *The Philokalia: The Complete Text*, vol. 4, translated by G. E. H. Palmer, Philip Sherrard, and Kallistos Ware (London: Faber & Faber, 1995).

"How Best to Say the Jesus Prayer" by Nicephoras the Solitary and "And the Faithful Shall Abide with Him" by Hesychius of Jerusalem are adapted from *Writings from the Philokalia on the Prayer of the Heart*, translated by E. Kadloubosky and G. E. H. Palmer (London: Faber & Faber, 1990).

"God's Word Is in All Creation" by Hildegard of Bingen is adapted from the translation by Matthew Fox in *The Coming of the Cosmic Christ* (New York: HarperCollins, 1988) © 1998 by Matthew Fox.

"To the Virgin" by Hildegard of Bingen is translated from the Latin by Andrew Harvey.

"On the Assumption" by Saint Bernard of Clairvaux is adapted from the translation by John Rotelle in *Meditations on Mary through the Ages* (Ann Arbor, Mich.: Redeemer Books).

"Mary, Star of the Sea" by Saint Bernard of Clairvaux is taken from the translation of Homily 2, on *Missus Est,* by Marie-Bernard Said in *Bernard of Clairvaux: Homilies in Praise of the Blessed Virgin Mary* (Kalamazoo, Mich.: Cistercian Publications).

"The Song of the Sun" by Saint Francis of Assisi is translated from the Italian by Andrew Harvey.

"How the Soul through the Senses Finds God in All Creatures" by Jacopone da Todi is taken from the translation by Serge and Elizabeth Hughes in *Jacopone da Todi: The Lauds* (Mahwah, N.J.: Paulist Press, 1982).

"God Speaks to the Soul" by Mechtild of Magdeburg is taken from *Beguine Spirituality,* edited by Fiona Bowie and translated by Oliver Davies (New York: Crossroad, 1989).

"To Live Out What I Am" and "Subject to that Great Power" by Hadewijch of Antwerp is taken from *Hade-*

wijch: The Complete Works, translated and introduced by Mother Columba Hart (Mahwah, N.J.: Paulist Press, 1980).

"Behold My Humility" by Angela of Foligno is adapted from the translation by Evelyn Underhill in *Mysticism* (London: Methuen, 1911).

"Seeing God in and with Darkness" by Angela of Foligno is taken from *Angela of Foligno: Complete Works*, translated by Paul Lachance (Mahwah, N.J.: Paulist Press, 1993).

"The Divine Birth" by Meister Eckhart is adapted from the translation by Jonathan Star in *Two Suns Rising* (New York: Bantam, 1991).

"The Spark and the Ground" and "Sermon Nineteen" by Meister Eckhart are taken from *Meister Eckhart: Sermons and Treatises*, vol. 3, translated and edited by M. O'C. Walshe (Rockport, Mass.: Element Books, 1979).

"The Vision of God" by Dante Alighieri is taken from *The Paradiso*, translated by John Ciardi (New York: Penguin, 1970).

"The Path of Pain" by Johannes Tauler is adapted from the translation by Evelyn Underhill in *Mysticism* (London: Methuen, 1911).

"My Sufferings are the Door"and "How Steadfastly One Must Fight Who Would Attain the Spiritual Prize" by Heinrich Suso are adapted from the translation by Frank Tobin in *Heinrich Suso: The Exemplar, with Two German Sermons* (Mahwah, N.J.: Paulist Press, 1985).

"Jesus, Are You Not My Mother" by Marguerite of Oingt is from her *Pagina Meditationum*, adapted from a translation by Caroline Walker Bynum.

"Christ the Mother" and "Every Sort of Thing Will Be All Right" by Julian of Norwich are adapted from *Julian of Norwich: Revelations of Divine Love*, translated by Clifton Wolters (New York: Penguin, 1966).

"The Soul as Living Mirror" by John Ruusbroec is adapted from *John Ruusbroec: The Spritual Espousals and Other Works*, translated by James Wiseman (Mahwah, N.J.: Paulist Press, 1985)

"Deified Souls" and "Both Work and Rest, Action and Fruition" by John Ruusbroec are adapted from the translation by Evelyn Underhill in *Mysticism* (London: Methuen, 1911).

"Me in You and You in Me" by Saint Catherine of Siena is adapted from the translation by Suzanne Noffke in

Catherine of Siena: The Dialogue (Mahwah, N.J.: Paulist Press, 1980).

"The Spiritual Marriage" and "Martha and Mary" by Saint Teresa of Ávila are taken from *The Interior Castle*, translated by Kieran Kavanaugh and Otilio Rodriguez (Mahwah, N.J.: Paulist Press, 1979).

"The Dark Night" by Saint John of the Cross is taken from *Saint John of the Cross: Poems*, translated by Willis Barnstone (New York: New Directions, 1972).

"The Purification of the Fire" by Saint John of the Cross is adapted from *The Living Flame of Love*, translated by E. Allison Peers (Burns and Oates, 1977).

"The Elixir" by George Herbert is taken from *George Herbert: The Collected Poems* (Oxford: Clarendon Press, 1958).

"The House of God" by Thomas Traherne is taken from *Thomas Traherne: Centuries, Poems, and Thanksgivings*, edited by H. M. Margoliuth (Oxford: Clarendon Press, 1958).

"The Knot" by Henry Vaughn is taken from *The Complete Poems of Henry Vaughn*, edited by French Fogle (New York: W. W. Norton, 1964).

"I Must Be the Virgin and Give Birth to God" is a series of epigrams by Angelius Silesius, translated from the German by Andrew Harvey.

"Dearest and Holiest and Most Beloved Mother" and "Mary and the Second Coming of Christ" by Saint Louis-Marie Grignon de Montfort; and "The Treasure" and "His Work Is Perfect" by Jean-Pierre de Causade are translated from the French by Andrew Harvey.

"To the Christians," "The Divine Image," and "Auguries of Innocence" by William Blake are taken from *William Blake: Collected Poems* (New York: Penguin, 1991).

"The Holy Conversation between Saint Seraphim of Sarov and Motovilov" by N. A. Motovilov is adapted from *A Wonderful Revelation to the World by Saint Seraphim*, translated by Archimandrite Lazarus Moore from *Orthodox Life*, vol. 4 (1953).

"The Magic of the Name of Jesus" is adapted from *The Way of a Pilgrim*, translated by R. M. French (New York: Seabury Press, 1965)

"True Christianity" by Vladimir Soloviev is adapted from a translation by Paul M. Allen in his *Vladimir Soloviev: Russian Mystic* (Baluvelt, N.Y.: Stiener Books, 1978).

"God's Grandeur" and the excerpt from "The Blessed Virgin Compared to the Air We Breathe" by Gerard Manley Hopkins are taken from *Gerard Manley Hopkins: Poems and Prose* (New York: Penguin, 1985).

"The Little Way" by Saint Thérèse of Lisieux is translated from the French by Andrew Harvey.

"Love's Vision" by Edward Carpenter is from his *Towards Democracy* (London: Allen and Unwin, 1883).

"The Cosmic Christ" by Pierre Tielhard de Chardin is adapted from *The Divine Milieu*, translated by Bernard Wall (New York: Harper and Row, 1960).

"A New Identity and a New Mode of Action" by Thomas Merton is taken from *The New Man* (New York: Farrar, Straus & Giroux, 1961).

"The Tradition of Praise" by Matthew Fox is taken from his *The Coming of the Cosmic Christ* (New York: Harper and Row, 1989) © 1989 by Matthew Fox.

"Being Happy with Him Now" by Mother Teresa of Calcutta is taken from *The Tibetan Book of Living and Dying* by Sogyal Rinpoche (New York: HarperCollins, 1992).

"The New Creation" by Bede Griffiths is taken from *A New Vision of Reality* (New York: HarperCollins, 1989).

"Envoi" by Saint Teresa of Ávila (said to be from a letter by Teresa to one of her nuns) is taken from Eknath Easwaran's *God Makes the Rivers to Flow* (Tomales, Calif.: Nilgiri Press, 1991), copyright 1975, Nilgiri Press, Tomales, CA 94971.